NORTH
SPAIN
COAST

T0247217

MARCO POLO
TOP HIGHLIGHTS

OVIEDO ⭐
The historic sights of the beautiful Asturian capital are a dream to discover on foot.
📷 *Tip: Head to a particular bench in the city park where cult comic character Mafalda is waiting to take a selfie with you.*

➤ p. 91, Asturias

BILBAO ⭐
Once a gritty industrial hub, this city has blossomed into a top tourist destination thanks to the Guggenheim effect.

➤ p. 50, Basque Country

SANTANDER ⭐
Cantabria's capital remains largely undiscovered by the tourist masses. So much the better for you – you can explore this elegant city in peace.

➤ p. 60, Cantabria

A CORUÑA ⭐
The *Ciudad de Cristal,* with its classic glass balconies, is home to possibly one of the most famous lighthouses in the world.
📷 *Tip: Be brave and climb those 234 steps up the Torre de Hércules; you can take the best pictures from the top.*

➤ p. 100, Galicia

GIJÓN ⭐
This Asturian port city, with its two beaches, might not be the prettiest place to visit, but it's so varied you'll never get bored.

➤ p. 76, Asturias

SANTILLANA DEL MAR ⭐ 8

If the queue for the Altamira Caves gets unbearable, head to the picturesque village nearby – although that too is a tourist trap!

➤ p. 67, Cantabria

SAN SEBASTIÁN ⭐ 2

Some say this Basque city nestled in the Bay of La Concha is the most beautiful city in the world. Go and see it for yourself – you won't find that notion so far-fetched (photo).

📷 *Tip: Take a picture of the Isla Santa Clara through the railings at La Concha beach to give your photo a really stylish frame!*

➤ p. 44, Basque Country

ISLAS CÍES ⭐

This group of islands feels almost like the Caribbean – turquoise water and "the most beautiful beach in the world".

➤ p. 114, Galicia

SANTIAGO DE COMPOSTELA ⭐ 7

This city is at the end of a pilgrimage route, the famous Way of St James, or *Camino de Santiago*. Keep an eye out for scallop shells!

📷 *Tip: Head to the Alameda Park at the edge of the city centre for a perfect view of the cathedral and old town.*

➤ p. 108, Galicia

PRAIA DAS CATEDRAIS ⭐ 10

This "Cathedral Beach" is truly a mythical place.

📷 *Tip: Take a walk around and you might find a spot where you can see several archways framed inside each other.*

➤ p. 108, Galicia

CONTENTS

CONTENTS

⏱ Plan your visit   🍴 Eating/drinking

€-€€€ Price categories   👜 Shopping

(*) Premium-rate   🍸 Going out
    phone number
                            🏖 Top beaches

(📖 A2) Refers to the removable pull-out map
(📖 a2) Additional map on the pull-out map
(📖 0) Off the pull-out map

Santa Catalina church, Mundaka

BEST OF THE NORTH SPAIN COAST

Cudillero in Asturias is a picture-book fishing village

BEST ☂
WHEN IT RAINS

ACTIVITIES TO BRIGHTEN YOUR DAY

**DON'T BE AFRAID OF
THE SHARKS**

The glass tunnel *Aquarium* in San Sebastián will keep you dry, even if it's raining cats and dogs outside. But you might end up drenched in sweat watching hungry-looking sharks cruising their tank (photo).

➤ p. 44, Basque Country

EXPLORE THE CAVES

The rock paintings in the *Cueva de Altamira* are stringently protected, meaning you can only visit a replica of the cave – unless you are incredibly lucky...

➤ p. 68, Cantabria

INTO THE UNDERWORLD

Head to the abandoned village of *Mina de Arnao* and visit the oldest coal mines on the Iberian Peninsula – and pray that sea water doesn't start leaking in like it did in 1915.

➤ p. 83, Asturias

SALUD!

When the weather's bad, why not drink away your troubles? Try a *cata*, an Albariño winetasting, at one of the many *bodegas* in the beautiful town of *Cambados*.

➤ p. 118, Galicia

**NOBEL PRIZE-WINNING
CHAMBER POTS**

The *Fundación Camilo José Cela* in Padrón is home to the Nobel Prize winner's substantial chamber pot collection. Oh, and his medals too.

➤ p. 119, Galicia

SHOP UNDER COVER

Even in awful weather, you won't need an umbrella to browse a covered market at your leisure. The ones in Bilbao, Santander and Oviedo, are especially fun.

➤ p. 52, p. 63, p. 91

BEST 🐷
ON A BUDGET

FOR SMALLER WALLETS

BARGAIN BITES
At the *pintxo-pote* (*pintxo bars*) in San Sebastián (usually on Thursdays) you can sample local cuisine paired with a delicious drink at discount prices (photo).
➤ p. 46, Basque Region

TOO CLOSE FOR COMFORT
At the *Ciudadela de Celestino Solar*, the only remaining settlement of this type in Gijón, you will experience up close what it was like for Asturian workers of the past to live with 11 other men in a 30m² shack.
➤ p. 77, Asturias

CLOCK IN
Despite its rather boring name, *Museo de los Relojes* (the clock museum) is actually a collection of antique timepieces located all around the city hall of A Coruña. It's a unique opportunity to visit the historic offices and assembly rooms instrumental to Galician politics. It doesn't cost a penny, but you will need to bring ID.
➤ p. 103, Galicia

DUSTY DRAWING ROOMS
Find out how Galician potters used to live in the 19th century at the *Ecomuseo Forno do Forte* in Buño. Here you can potter around some historic potter's rooms and even make your own pot – all for free.
➤ p. 108, Galicia

A GOTHIC ENTHUSIAST'S DREAM
The ruins of the medieval church of Santa Mariña de Dozo stretch into the sky at the heart of the melancholy *cemetery* in the Galician wine town of *Cambados*. Eerily beautiful, extremely romantic; free entry.
➤ p. 118, Galicia

BEST WITH CHILDREN

FUN FOR YOUNG & OLD

ROLLERCOASTER RIDE ON A CLIFF EDGE

The funicular railway in San Sebastián, which is over 100 years old, will take you up the steep *Monte Igueldo* to the amusement park high up on the mountain, where you can zoom along the brink of a precipice on a rollercoaster. Not for scaredy cats!

➤ p. 44, Basque Country

SMALL TALK WITH SEA LIONS

Little animal lovers can peek at plunging penguins and chat with the sea lions at the *Parque Marino* on La Magdalena Peninsula in Santander. Yes, they answer back. Try it and see!

➤ p. 62, Cantabria

ALL HOUSES GREAT & SMALL

The grounds of the *Muséu del Pueblu d'Asturies* in Gijón are full of historic houses for you to explore – from meagre shepherds' huts to mansions.

➤ p. 80, Asturias

ALIEN EGGS & DINOSAURS

The building of the *Museo del Jurásico de Asturias MUJA* (photo) looks like a clutch of huge eggs laid by aliens. Inside, you can learn everything you ever wanted to know about prehistoric creatures and even – ahem – see a pair of T-Rex skeletons having sex. Good luck explaining that one!

➤ p. 87, Asturias

PLAY AT BEING EXPLORERS

In Baiona, you can climb on the replica of the caravel-type ship *La Pinta* and get an idea of how hard it must have been to go on a sea voyage in Columbus's day. *La Pinta* was the first of the three caravels to return to Europe.

➤ p. 114, Galicia

BEST

CLASSIC EXPERIENCES

ONLY ON THE NORTH SPAIN COAST

TRADITIONAL INSTRUMENT

At the *Museo de la Gaita* in Gijón, you can take a look at Asturias's version of bagpipes. But Asturians readily admit they aren't the only ones to come up with a similar instrument.

➤ p. 80, Asturias

FAITH OR SUPERSTITION?

Santiago de Compostela may be one of the most quintessentially Catholic cities in the world, but regular Galicians tend to put their trust in powers other than God. And what better proof than the protective amulets in *Santo André de Teixido*, which are made from dough?

➤ p. 107, Galicia

COFFINS IN THE GARDEN?

In Asturias, they're square and look a bit like treehouses. In Galicia, they're narrow with stilts and a cross on top and look like stone sarcophagi. They often have a kind of stake sticking out of the top. But these *hórreos* are not used to kill vampires. They're actually granaries, used to store corn and cereals. The most famous ones can be found in *Carnota*.

➤ p. 110, Galicia

CAUTION, HORSES CROSSING!

You're driving down a Galician coastal road when suddenly a *free-roaming herd* of horses cuts you up? That's totally normal here! And in the Picos de Europa you'll even see goats and donkeys too (photo).

SHOWBOATING ON THE SAND

Spanish city-dwellers often like to show off their (newly purchased) threads, especially along the beach *promenades*. Men wear jumpers slung round their shoulders; women wear heels, no matter how bumpy the cobblestones. But, don't parade about in your swimsuit unless you want to out yourself as a tourist.

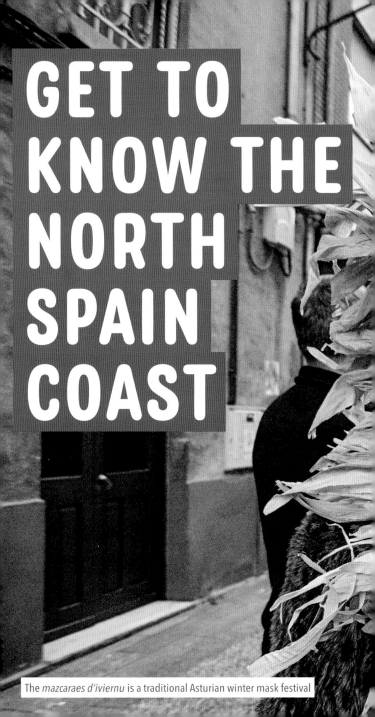

GET TO KNOW THE NORTH SPAIN COAST

The *mazcaraes d'iviernu* is a traditional Asturian winter mask festival

DISCOVER THE NORTH SPAIN COAST

The number one destination in Galicia is Santiago de Compostela

The North Spain Coast has everything in abundance – apart from tourists that is. That's down to the temperamental weather and the fact that hardly any holiday airlines fly there. Lucky you! You'll have endless beaches, lofty mountain ranges, medieval towns and chic seaside resorts practically all to yourself – along with the locals, who are friendly despite the harsh maritime climate.

JEALOUSY IN THE HINTERLAND
You've got gentility in Santander, beauty in San Sebastián, heartiness in Vigo and wonder in A Coruña. All the cities on the Atlantic coast of Northern Spain have one thing in common: they have a close relationship with the sea and with their maritime origins.

Around 35,000–15,000 BCE
Pre-historic man creates rock art in the Cave of Altamira

Around 7th century BCE
Celtic settlements in Asturias and Galicia

CE 218–201
Second Punic War, Romans defeat the Carthaginians to conquer the Iberian Peninsula

5th century
Suebi and Visigoths take over the region

711
Start of the Moorish conquest of the Iberian Peninsula

718
The Christian reconquest, *La Reconquista*, begins in Asturias under Pelayo

It's only natural that the venerable towns of the hinterlands are a little jealous. The Galician town of Pontevedra may boast a picture-perfect medieval city centre, but does it have that beach atmosphere and the squawk of seagulls? Not a chance. The Asturian city of Oviedo, with its historic centre and cathedral with only one tower (because there wasn't enough money for more) is filled with students, which ensures a relaxed atmosphere, but it doesn't have a sea breeze. Bilbao, once a grey industrial eyesore and denounced as the ugly duckling of the Basque Country, has blossomed into a magnificent swan thanks to the Guggenheim Museum – but anyone attempting to take a dip on the banks of the Río Nervión will be sorely disappointed. No wonder the *bilbaínos* are jealous of their long-time rival San Sebastián, which boasts no less than three beaches. Last but not least, there's the world-renowned city of Santiago de Compostela: how annoying to be a pilgrim and trudge hundreds of miles along the Way of St James and be unable to dunk your throbbing feet in the cool, refreshing sea at the end of it. Instead, you have to queue up in the cathedral to kiss a statue of a saint.

MOUNTAIN GETAWAYS

And the hinterlands themselves? You think you're in Spain, and then you find yourself in the middle of forest-covered hills. These hills are studded with little farmsteads, many of which are half-timbered houses with sheep grazing in front of them. So much for the Basque Country. Head a little further west to Cantabria

1492
End of *La Reconquista*

1936-1939
Spanish Civil War, start of the Franco dictatorship

1959
Basque group ETA founded

1975
Death of Franco, Spain becomes parliamentary monarchy

2018
Dissolution of ETA

2020
Spain suffers greatly due to the coronavirus pandemic, tourism comes to a standstill

2023
Tour de France starts in Bilbao

and Asturias and things get even more unsettling with the towering Picos de Europa making you feel as if you're in the Alps. The mountains are snow-capped, even in summer. And they're dotted with countless caves, some with internationally famous rock paintings daubed on the walls, while others are filled with the smelliest cheese in the whole of Spain. But sunseekers need not worry: the coast is never far away – even when you're in the mountains; most of the cloud-covered summits are just a few kilometres from the nearest *playa*.

"BUT THAT'S SO FAR AWAY!"

The weather is the main reason foreign tourists have tended to snub Northern Spain as a holiday destination. If, for example, you ask someone in Gijón whether they get many visitors from abroad, they'll chuckle and say, oh, it's usually just Spanish people, and those only come between June and September. In smaller towns, if you tell people where you're from, they'll look at you, confused, and say, "You're British? But that's so far away!" This means that, outside the Spanish holiday season, you often have mile-long beaches practically all to yourself; that also applies to some of the main attractions, even during peak times.

FAR FROM PASSIONLESS

While the southern European countries are generally considered to be full of fiery-eyed Carmens and passionate *toreros*, the northern Spaniards are accused of being a little cooler – probably in part because of the weather. But that couldn't be more wrong! This will become immediately apparent if you go to a pub to watch one of their football teams playing in Primera División, the Spanish equivalent of the English Premier League. Sparks fly, and the spectators scream, shout and sweat along with the players. And you'll see the same level of excitement on an evening of bar hopping and tapas. The animated discussions are seldom arguments – although they may sound that way. They're usually about food, family, furniture or the weather. Occasionally, they're about politics, but only the stuff from the present that they can laugh about.

It's probably best to leave the country's political past well alone. Thorny topics, like the decades-long Franco dictatorship and the Basque group ETA, are by no means water under the bridge and the wounds have not yet healed. If you still want to know about the Northern Spain separatist movement, read *Patria* by Fernando Aramburu. After you have read this novel of the century, you'll understand once and for all the idiosyncrasies of Basque nationalism and its consequences. Apart from that, the people of Northern Spain are very peaceful – and extremely helpful. If you lose your way in the winding streets of an old town and ask a local the way, they might, instead of giving directions, come along with you and show you the way.

AT A GLANCE

6,509,000
inhabitants

Scotland: 5,480,000

"PRÍNCIPE/PRINCESA DE ASTURIAS"

Title for the heir to the Spanish throne (since 2014: Leonor de Borbón e Ortiz)

260

Number of wild bears in the Cantabrian mountains

52,733km²
surface area

Republic of Ireland: 70,273km²

HIGHEST MOUNTAIN: TORRE DE CERREDO

2,648m

in the Picos de Europa in Asturias

ANNUAL VISITORS TO THE GUGGENHEIM MUSEUM

1,266,000

Tate Britain
1,500,000

FOOTBALL TEAMS IN THE PRIMERA DIVISIÓN

3

of which 2 are from the Basque Country (22/23 season)

7 UNESCO WORLD HERITAGE SITES

Monuments in the Oviedo old town and surroundings, Puente Bizkaia, the old town in Santiago de Compostela, Torre de Hércules in A Coruña, Altamira cave and other caves, pilgrimage routes to Santiago, Santimamiñe cave

FAMOUS PEOPLE

Fernando Alonso (racing driver), Ignacio de Loyola (order founder), Camilo José Cela (winner of the Nobel Prize for Literature), Francisco Franco (dictator), Letizia (queen)

66
Michelin stars
including four three-star restaurants in the Basque Country alone

UNDERSTAND THE NORTH SPAIN COAST

LANGUAGE CHAOS

We're almost used to the calls for Catalan independence and the fact that the Catalan language is favoured in Catalonia. It's also well known that the Basques are no longer fighting violently for their independence, but still cherish the Basque language as a sign of their self-sufficiency. But it comes as more of a surprise to find that the regional languages of Galicia and Asturias – much more similar to the Spanish national language of Castilian – are also systematically included in museum signage, on restaurant menus and street signs.

The variety of languages along the coast of Northern Spain posed problems for the editors and cartographers of this Marco Polo guide. Taking a strictly uniform approach – always opting for the Castilian variant or always using the regional spelling – would have been rather unhelpful for people just trying to find their way around. So, we have tried to use the variant that is most commonly found in the local area. And when it comes to names like San Sebastián/Donostia, we have chosen the variant that will be most familiar to an international audience.

INDIANA HOMES!

They might be known as "Indians", but they're not from the Asian subcontinent: *indianos* was the name used for emigrants in the mid-19th to mid-20th century who left their homeland (usually Asturias) and travelled to Latin America to make their fortune. Having filled their pockets and been overcome by homesickness, these *indianos* came home and built extravagant villas and estates. Several of the *casas indianas* or *casas de los indianos* are still standing today, and some of them are open to visitors. The most impressive property can be found in the town of Colombres, where you can walk in the footsteps of "Indians" and visit the "Indian" museum. But there are other places too. Keep your eyes peeled: as well as the architecture (which isn't always ostentatious), you can recognise these buildings by the palm tree beside the door.

> **INSIDER TIP**
> Spot the *casa indiana*!

SANTIAGO IS ALL THE RAGE

Since the turn of the century, the numbers of pilgrims walking the legendary Way of St James or *Camino de Santiago* has shot up. But *The* Way doesn't actually exist. In fact, there are seven official routes leading to Santiago de Compostela, a dream destination for soul-searchers. The most popular of these routes, the Camino Francés, is favoured by almost two-thirds of walkers because it isn't as strenuous as, for example, the Camino del Norte. But die-hard experts claim that the Way of St James along the coast is the one true route. Once you've done that, try one of the 39 other pilgrimages on the Iberian Peninsula. In recent years, well over 300,000 pilgrims have had their pilgrim passports stamped at their destination of Santiago del Compostela every year.

PEOPLE, PLAYAS & PLASTICS

Not for nothing does the Galician "Death Coast" bear its name. For hundreds of years, ships have been dashed to smithereens in the stormy and treacherous waters of the Costa da Morte. And the days of mourning the loss of vessels, cargo and human lives continued into the 20th century. In 1976, the Spanish tanker *Urquiola* ran aground on the rocks by A Coruña, dumping almost 100,000 tonnes of oil into the water. Just two years later, the Greek vessel *Andros Patria* exploded, costing 34 sailors their lives and dumping 50,000 tonnes of oil. In 1992, the Greek tanker *Aegean Sea* continued this tragic trend when it hit a reef and was smashed, dumping 75,000 tonnes of crude oil and polluting 300km of coast.

No sooner had nature had a chance to recover than the Greek tanker *Prestige* sprang a leak in 2002, discharging 60,000 tonnes of oil and causing the most catastrophic oil spill in European history, spreading pollution as far as France. This was partly because the Spanish government waited for days before sending help. Today, you don't need an oil slick to have environmentalists tearing their hair out. There's the disastrous

More than 300,000 pilgrims walk the *Camino de Santiago* each year.

The opening of Bilbao's Guggenheim Museum kick-started a boom in the Basque Country

invasion of microplastics, and coastlines littered with plastic bottles, car tyres, rubber boots and whatever else people see fit to toss in the ocean. The maritime museums and aquariums along the coast are now addressing the problem with displays of rubbish, hoping to mobilise visitors to become more environmentally aware.

THE GUGGENHEIM EFFECT

This term refers to the uptick in tourism, and the associated economic boom, that the industrial city of Bilbao in the Basque Country experienced after the opening of Frank Gehry's Guggenheim Museum in 1997. I'd like some of that, thought the Asturians, and commissioned Brazilian architect Oscar Niemeyer to build the Centro Niemeyer in the

run-down industrial town of Avilés. But since its opening in 2011, the cultural centre, which looks like a cross between a UFO and half a hen's egg, has failed to produce the desired "Niemeyer Effect". In a seemingly concerted effort not to learn from others' mistakes, the Centro Botín in the Cantabrian capital Santander opened in 2017. The prospects for success of this cultural centre are still anybody's guess, despite the artworks placed outside the doors to tempt people inside, a tactic that was successful in Bilbao. And what about Galicia? Have the Galicians been looking to create their own Guggenheim Effect? Well, yes, they have actually: construction of the Ciudad de la Cultura on Monte Gaiás in Santiago, designed by US architect Peter Eisenman, began in

2001. The first buildings were inaugurated in 2011, but the whole thing was temporarily halted in 2013. Work on the sprawling complex continues to this day. Will the city of culture ever be finished? Who knows.

THE GRASS IS ALWAYS GREENER

After a few canny tourism experts came up with the name Costa Verde, or "Green Coast", in the late 1960s as a way of marketing the Asturian coast, all the other northern regions thought this was a great idea and followed suit. Now, in addition to the Green Coast, we also have the slogan *España Verde*, or "Green Spain", which covers the Basque Country, Cantabria, Asturias and Galicia. And it's true that here in the north, with its harsh and rainy climate (by Spanish standards) and its hilly hinterlands, it is much greener than in the steppe-like Castile or baking-hot Andalucía. Instead of bulls, dairy cows roam the meadows that often stretch to the shore, idly watching beachgoers while chewing the cud.

The four regions together have some 2,000km of coastline. According to a survey in the newspaper *El País*, three of the five most beautiful beaches in Spain are in the north of the country: the Playa de Rodas on the Galician Islas Cíes near Vigo; the stunning Praia das Catedrais with its rock formations, which is also in Galicia and which the *Guardian* newspaper once named the most beautiful beach in the world; and La Concha beach in the Basque city of San Sebastián.

TRUE OR FALSE?

SPANIARDS ARE LOUD

That goes for northerners too. That's just the way it is. So if you like your peace and quiet when you're on holiday, if you don't like hearing shouting or plates clattering when you're at the pub, if you don't want constant car horns blaring and loud conversations, if you need your beauty sleep without noise outside the window, then don't forget your ear plugs!

SANTANDER IS TOO SPANISH!

This derogatory remark can be heard in Asturias, the Basque Country and Galicia. And by Santander they mean Cantabria, the smallest region in the north, of which Santander is the capital. The Cantabrians are known for their use of formal language and their love of bullfighting. They have never so much as mentioned independence, which is why there are rumours among the neighbours that Cantabria is a die-hard hotbed of fascism. But perhaps their prejudice is really caused by envy of the Cantabrians' noble, calm reserve and unflappability – including when it comes to politics. And its neighbours would do well to remember that Franco was Galician and holidayed in the Basque Country.

ON FALANGISTS & SEPARATISTS

There is more than one region in Spain that is notorious for freedom fighting, but it was the Basque Country organisation ETA (for its Basque name *Euskadi Ta Askatasuna*, or "Basque Country and Freedom") that was responsible for many deaths between its founding in 1959 and its official dissolution in 2018. No wonder this traumatic past is still as present as ever, especially since some segments of the population don't consider the *Etarras* to be criminals, but instead revere them as freedom fighters.

Another case of the past coming back to haunt us, this time of a fascist variety, is the notorious Galician Francisco Franco, the rebel general and dictator of Spain between 1936 and 1975. While there is no longer an equestrian statue of the "Generalísimo" in the Plaza de España in the Galician town of Ferrol, the house where he was born still displays several commemorative plaques reminding us of the Falangist dictator – whom many Galicians did not see as such a terrible dictator after all.

MEDIEVAL MIGRATION

The subject of so much strife would have elicited no more than a weary smile back in the Early Middle Ages. In CE 711, a Moor named Tarik succeeded in crossing from Ceuta in North Africa to Europe with a retinue of 7,000 men. He proceeded to lay claim to a rocky outcrop: the Jabal al-Tariq. This "Rock of Tariq" (a name that morphed only slightly to become Gibraltar) was the launchpad for an

unprecedented military campaign: in just under seven years the Muslims had occupied almost the entire Iberian Peninsula.

Not that the Christians took this lying down; just a decade later, they set out on a campaign to win Spain back under the legendary slogan *Reconquista* ("reconquest"), with the equally legendary Battle of Covadonga in the Asturian Picos de Europa. The commander of the troops at the time was a certain King Pelayo who, after winning the battle, founded the Asturian Empire and with it the

The joy of Green Spain: mountain walking in the morning; sea swimming in the afternoon

first Christian bastion on the road to reconquest. Keep your eyes peeled: you'll encounter Pelayo (who has acquired cult status) at every turn – even though the *Reconquista* took 700 years in the end. It was not until 1492 that the Moors were finally defeated in Spain.

URSINE OBSERVATION?

In Asturias, there is a fairly large and well-protected brown bear population, and they can also be found in Cantabria. The animals are incredibly shy, making an encounter an unlikely occurrence. The Asturian hiking trail Senda del Oso ("Bear Trail"), which follows a disused railway line, takes you via an observation station to a bear enclosure, featuring the bears Paca and Molina. On the other hand, in the villages around Oviedo they claim that the bears are not a bit shy, but quite curious, and sometimes come out of the mountains within sight of the towns to see what people are up to.

EATING
SHOPPING
SPORT

Shellfish, including *almejas* (clams), are bountiful along the Atlantic coast

EATING & DRINKING

If the weather is preventing you from sizzling in the sun all day, why not try something sizzling from the stove instead? Basque cuisine is considered the best in all of Spain. And with around 40 Michelin stars, the Basques have more stars per capita than anywhere else in the world except for Kyoto, Japan.

ATTRACTING CUSTOMERS OR PROTECTING FROM FLIES?

Spain's most famous culinary delicacy is the tapa. The origin of the custom of pairing alcoholic drinks with nibbles is the stuff of legend – or several legends. The oldest dates back to the 13th century. The story goes that the ailing King Alfonso X was advised by his personal physician to eat all his meals in tiny portions, a recommendation that the savvy monarch passed on to his subjects. Other sources claim that, in the 15th century, the Catholic sovereigns Fernando and Isabel decreed that all the taverns in the land could only serve alcohol accompanied by small dishes because the people were too often three sheets to the wind. The most persistent theory is that it was a southern Spanish waiter who once covered a beer glass with a small plate of olives. Opinion is divided as to whether this was done to attract customers or to protect the drink from thirsty flies. But we do know that the term tapa originates from the Spanish word tapar, meaning "to cover".

STRIPTEASE & LITTLE STICKS

As is so often the case, the Basques do things a bit differently when it comes to tapas. Here, the small plates of food are known as pintxos, after the little wooden sticks with which the creations are skewered. The "mother of all pintxos" called Gilda, probably

Regional delicacies: tasty *pintxos* (left) and pungent *cabrales* (right)

originates from the 1940s at the Casa Vallés bar in San Sebastián. The skewer, studded with anchovies, peppers and olives, was said to be so spicy that it prompted one guest to compare it to American actress Rita Hayworth's steamy glove striptease in the 1946 film *Gilda*. Nevertheless, the restaurant Casa Lita (which only opened in 2003) in the Cantabrian city of Santander has a sign by the bar claiming that the dish was invented there – and there are others too. The story of the Gilda's origin is most likely a mishmash of truth and fiction.

Incidentally – and this goes for both tapas and *pintxos* – the days when a chef would just throw together a few olives are long gone. Now, you see all kinds of exotic and experimental creations. The best way to get an overview of this culinary art form is to do what the

INSIDER TIP
Bar crawl for foodies

Basques call *txikiteo* and others call *tapeo*: hopping from bar to bar and trying a different *tapa* (plus drink) at each stop along the way.

SOUPED UP

With all the culinary prowess Northern Spain's modern cuisine has to offer, it's easy to forget that its origins are anything but noble. The north of the Iberian Peninsula was once extremely poor, and the women of the house often had their work cut out feeding the hungry mouths of their often-large families. A good way to do this was with hearty soups and stews, the most fabled of which have survived to the present day. In the Basque Country, these are called *marmitako* and are primarily made with fish (especially tuna) and potatoes; their Cantabrian neighbours swear by *cazuelas*, fish stews usually featuring hake and anchovies. The Asturians favour *fabada*, a stew made from white kidney beans and every cut of pork the cook can get their hands on; the Galicians have their *caldo galego*, a soup made of cabbage, potatoes, bacon and turnips.

SEÑORES AT THE STOVE
Most of the Michelin-starred celebrity chefs of the *Nueva Cocina Vasca* are men – take, for example, Martín Berasategui, Pedro Subijana and Juan Mari Arzak (though this cooking legend from San Sebastián shares the limelight with his daughter Elena). One reason for this can be found in the traditional Basque *txokos*, gastronomical societies that are exclusively for men. Women only have access to these traditional clubs as guests, and never in the kitchen. The first of these *sociedades gastronómicas* was founded in the late 19th century when the men sought out a place where they could meet for a chat and a drink. Then they had the idea of creating these cooking clubs… Today, there are around 130 in San Sebastián alone.

WHAT SHOULD YOU DRINK IF YOU'RE UNDE-CIDER-ED?
Good wine needs a mild climate and sun-drenched slopes! The rugged Galician weather suits the fresh white wines Ribeiro and Albariño, and the Basque Country's answer to good wine is Txakoli, a dry sparkling vino that is poured from a height. Then there's the Spanish *sidra*, or cider. They are particularly fond of it in Asturias, where some streets are filled with rows upon rows of *sidrerías*. If you prefer something a bit livelier, why not try the Galician pomace brandy *orujo*, which can sometimes reach 50% alcohol content. According to many, the tastiest beers are Estrella Galicia, from Galicia, or Keler, the traditional Basque beer from San Sebastián.

WHEN DOES IT ALL HAPPEN?
Spaniards are late risers and night owls. Everything in the day happens around two hours later than it does for most of their European neighbours. People seldom meet at a bar for their first *cortado* – a small, strong coffee with a dash of frothy milk – before 10am. Lunch is between 1pm and 2pm at the very earliest, and if you show up to a restaurant for dinner at 8.30pm, you certainly won't encounter any locals there – they always eat late. Many restaurants will still serve you a juicy *chuletón* (a huge T-bone ox steak) at midnight. And at dawn, after a night of partying, you can indulge in *chocolate con churros*: thick cocoa with sticks or twists of dough fried in oil.

Today's specials

Pescados y Mariscos

ANCHOAS DE SANTOÑA
Cantabrian anchovies

BOGAVANTE DE SAN VICENTE DE LA BARQUERA
Cantabrian lobster

KOKOTXAS
Fish cheeks

MERLUZA EN SALSA VERDE
Hake in green sauce

OSTRAS DE VIGO
Galician oysters

RODABALLO
Turbot

MEJILLONES
Mussels

NAVAJAS
Razor clams

PULPO A FEIRA
Boiled octopus with paprika and potatoes

FABES CON ALMEJAS
White kidney beans with clams

VIEIRAS GRATINADAS
Scallop gratin

Carnes

COCIDO MONTAÑÉS
Cantabrian bean stew with bacon and pork

LACÓN CON GRELOS
Ham hock with greens

FILETE DE TERNERA
Veal escalope

CHULETON DE TXOGITXU
Thick T-bone steak (from older cows)

Postres

ARROZ CON LECHE ASTURIANO
Rice pudding with caramelised sugar crust

QUESADA PASIEGA
Spanish cheesecake

FRIXUELOS
Asturian crêpes

SHOPPING

LOOKING FOR SOME MAGIC?

We've all experienced painful ailments, troubles at work or problems with a relationship. Well, there just so happens to be a perfect remedy close at hand. The manufacturing company Sargadelos *(sargadelos.com)*, which is located in the village of the same name and is known for Its porcelain, produces amulets and charms to protect against theft, boost the libido and ward off witches. If that's not enough, you can head to Santo André de Teixido where the talismans made of bread dough, known as *sanandresiños*, are guaranteed to keep your worries at bay – so long as you believe in them.

ONLY THE DUTCH WEAR CLOGS? NONSENSE!

In the countryside of Northern Spain people used to wear wooden clogs to go out in the fields. It's a pity that, at a certain point, rubber welly boots made their triumphant advance and booted the clunky clogs out of the limelight, even in rural Galicia. This meant that, in order to survive, producers of these *zocos*, known as *zoqueiros*, had to find creative solutions. The Ferro family, for instance, began producing designer *zocos*. These shoes, with their wooden soles and colourful leather uppers, are a bit of a hidden gem for avant-garde fashionistas. All the materials are made in Pontevedra, but you can also buy them from a shop in A Coruña *(elenaferro.com)*.

INSIDER TIP
Stylish clogs for fashionistas

HATS, BALLS & CHEESE

The classic Basque beret worn by fishing folk and farmers alike is back in fashion. They are worn at celebrations or by tourists in summer and by hip

Northern Spain is full of surprises, from Galician clogs to Asturian cider

locals strolling through the city during rainy winter days. And you can find them in all different colours! Don't believe us? The Netflix series *Emily in Paris* may be a little foolish, but it did bring the traditional *txapela* (or *boina* in Spanish) back in style.

The sporty ones among you might prefer to purchase a Basque *pelota* ball – and make sure you get some racquets too.

Or you could bring back the Basque Country's most popular product: the delicious Idiazábal cheese. Just make sure it's shrink-wrapped to keep the smell from escaping.

WATCH OUT FOR SPILLS!

From the French to the Portuguese border, Northern Spain goes nuts for cider. Asturians are the most known for their *sidra*, but the Basques, Galicians and Cantabrians produce some delicious tipples too – and

stocking your suitcases won't break the bank. But there's a catch: the cider only tastes at its best when it has been poured from a height. You're better off taking it outside if you fancy trying this at home.

CAN-DO ATTITUDE!

Cantabria is famous for the quality of its seafood. But you can hardly pack a lobster or a dozen oysters in your luggage. Why not take some anchovies home instead? The best ones come from Santoña, halfway between Bilbao and Santander, where they have been canning them for generations. They won't spill in your suitcase, they last forever, and some of the tins are so pretty that you can keep them as ornaments.

SPORT & ACTIVITIES

The Atlantic coast of Northern Spain is a real surfers' paradise. But caution, windsurfers: we don't mean you! We mean the real tough cookies who ride the waves without a sail to help them. If you want to stay dry, you're better off going hiking – it's rarely too hot for that up here in the north. Beyond the Way of St James, there are many less-trodden paths along the coast or through the Picos de Europa mountain range. You can also hike from hole to hole on one of the beautiful and/or fashionable golf courses that are often lauded for their stunning sea views.

CYCLING & MOUNTAIN BIKING

You can rent bikes in all major cities, and some companies also offer guided cycling tours of the sights. If you would rather stick to the countryside, we recommend the *vías verdes* (viasverdes.com): cycling routes built on disused or railway lines. You can also pedal along the coastal *Camino del Norte*, one of the routes of the Way of St James, either on your own or as part of an organised excursion. Important: helmets are compulsory across the whole of Spain in built-up areas and for anyone under the age of 16. Mountain bikers can find MTB centres all over the country. The Basque Country alone has a route network of 1,500km. You can also rent mountain bikes. Head to the local tourist information centre or visit *centrosbtt.es* for further details.

GOLF

With its green rolling hills and meadows all along the coast, it's hardly surprising that Northern Spain is a dream golfing destination. Just don't hit your ball into the sea! Some of the best courses are listed below. For a

The left-hand point break at Mundaka is an iconic wave for serious surfers

traditional club dating back to 1916 with nine holes and a beautiful sea view, check out *Real Golf Club de Zarauz (tel. 9 43 83 01 45 | golfzarauz. com)* in Zarautz. The 18-hole *Real Nuevo Club Golf de San Sebastián Basozabal (tel. 9 43 46 76 42 | golf basozabal.com)* is located on a challenging slope in the hills behind San Sebastián. The nine-hole course at *Club de Golf Mataleñas (tel. 9 42 39 27 75 | golfmatalenas.com)* in Santander is considered one of the most beautiful in Spain because of its incredible views of the beach and ocean. The 18-hole *Golf Santa Marina (tel. 9 42 71 00 49 | golfsantamarina.es)* set against the backdrop of snow-capped mountain peaks in San Vicente de la Barquera, was designed by golfing legend Severiano Ballesteros. The 18-hole course *Golf Municipal de Llanes (tel. 9 85 41 72 30 | llanes.es/golf)* in Llanes overlooks the sea and the Sierra del Cuera. In Gijón, many slanting slopes and old clusters of trees await at the 18-hole *Real Club de Golf de Castiello (tel. 9 85 36 63 13 | castiello.com)*. For a beautiful 18-hole course with plenty of water hazards, be sure to visit *Real Club de Golf de La Coruña (tel. 9 81 28 52 00 | clubgolfcoruna.com)* in A Coruña. *Golf La Toja (tel. 9 86 73 01 58 | latojagolf.com)* in O Grove boasts a nine-hole course on the fancy Illa da Toxa in the Ría de Arousa.

HIKING

It's all about the Way of St James. There are seven official variants, with 39 additional routes on the Iberian Peninsula alone. The most popular and easiest route is the *Camino Francés*, but insiders swear by the considerably more challenging coastal route, the *Camino del Norte*, which is far less busy as a result. You can find further information about routes, stages and everything else you need to know at *www.pilgrim.es.*

On the other hand, the Picos de Europa are right round the corner. For an incredibly beautiful – and not too tiring – experience, why not take a tour to the Asturian mountain lakes Lago de Enol and Lago de la Ercina in Covadonga. If you would prefer a sea view, Santoña in Cantabria boasts several trails with panoramic views that lead up and around Monte Buciero, leading to fortifications and lighthouses (for further information, check out *farodelcaballo.es*). And all along the miles and miles of coastline, you can find regional and local paths, most of which are well maintained, with incredible views (and incredible beaches). One example is the *Ruta de las Playas* in Ribadeo, Galicia, leading to the *Praia das Catedrais*, which is one of the most beautiful beaches in Spain *(turismo.ribadeo.gal).*

KAYAKING & CANOEING

Away from the coast in the Picos de Europa you will find prime conditions for watersports amid picture-perfect scenery on the Río Sella. You can take short excursions or day trips by canoe or kayak in the areas around Cangas de Onís and Arriondas using providers such as *Cangas Aventura (Arriondas: Finca la Dehesa | tel. 9 85 84 16 99; Cangas de Onís: Av. Covadonga 17 | tel. 9 85 84 92 61 | cangasaventura.com)* or *Aventura Norte (Arriondas | C/ Pozo Barreño B2 | tel. 6 36 25 89 43 | multi aventuranorte.es)*, which also offers

rafting tours on the river. But if nothing but the ocean will do, you can rent kayaks to explore places such as the sheltered Ondarreta beach in San Sebastián from companies like *Alokayak (Playa de Ondarreta | tel. 6 46 11 27 47 | alokayak.com).* Or if you fancy exploring Cantabria, try *Yumping (Av. Severiano Ballesteros | tel. 9 17 90 79 09 | yumping.com)* in Santander. And *Aventuras en Galicia (tel. 9 81 56 17 85 | aventurasen galicia.com)* offers several rental centres in Galicia.

PELOTA 🏳

The traditional sport played in Northern Spain is the Basque game of *pelota*. You'll find *pelota* courts all over the place; they're free to use and you can buy a ball and racquets cheaply at most sports shops. How does it work? Just copy the locals. Or simply hit the ball against the wall with the racquet. Purists do it with their bare hands – but we don't advise that unless you've been playing *pelota* all your life.

INSIDER TIP
Play at being a real Basque

SURFING

The whole of the coast of Northern Spain is one big surf spot. You can sign up for lessons or simply rent a board from one of the course providers. Here are a few select providers, listed from east to west.

Trial lessons, courses and boards to rent are on offer from *Zurriola Surf Eskola (C/ Usandizaga 14 | tel. 9 43 01 13 91 | zurriolasurfeskola.com)* in San Sebastián. On the Playa de

Zarautz in the Basque Country, which offers a good 2km of beach, *Pukas Surf (C/ Lizardi 9 | tel. 9 43 89 06 36 | eskola.pukassurf.com)* is the top dog. In Mundaka, the place with the world-famous lefthander wave, *Mundaka Barra Surf (C/ Basamortu 6 | tel. 6 88 77 26 22 | mundakabarra surf.com)* offers courses and camps.

On Santander's Playa Sardinero, head to *Escuela de Surf Sardinero (Balneario 1a | tel. 9 42 27 03 01 | escueladesurfsardinero.com)* or *Escuela de Surf Santander (C/ Dr. Marañón | tel. 6 69 48 80 14 | escueladesurf santander.com)* for surfing and surf-board rental. In Laredo, *Escuela de Surf Pinos Laredo (Av. Enrique Mowinkel 57 | tel. 6 87 25 63 87 | escuelasurfpinoslaredo.com)* also offers stand-up paddleboarding lessons.

For surfing in the city, try *Skoolsurf (Av. Rufo García Rendueles 15 | tel. 9 85 36 84 43 | skoolsurf.com)* in Gijón. In surfing hotspot Salinas, the *Escuela de Surf Long Beach (C/ Piñole 20 | tel. 6 51 95 88 29 | escuelade surflongbeach.com)* also offers camps.

In the less-touristy region of Northern Galicia, try *Escuela Gallega de Surf (Playa de Esteiro | tel. 6 27 97 96 38 | escuelagallegadesurf.es)* in Viveiro. It's busier at *Galisurf (Rúa Menéndez y Pelayo 5 | tel. 6 79 55 47 93 | galisurf.es)* in the major city of A Coruña.

The Picos de Europa are ideal for hiking

REGIONAL OVERVIEW

On the Costa Verde, the cows watch you when you go to the beach

Gijón/
Xixón

Ferrol

A Coruña

GALICIA p. 96

Oviedo/
Uviéu

ASTURIAS

Lugo

Santiago de
Compostela

Pontevedra

Ourense

Vigo

Windswept capes, appealing cities, countless beaches and abundant seafood

PORTUGAL

ESPAÑA

Douro

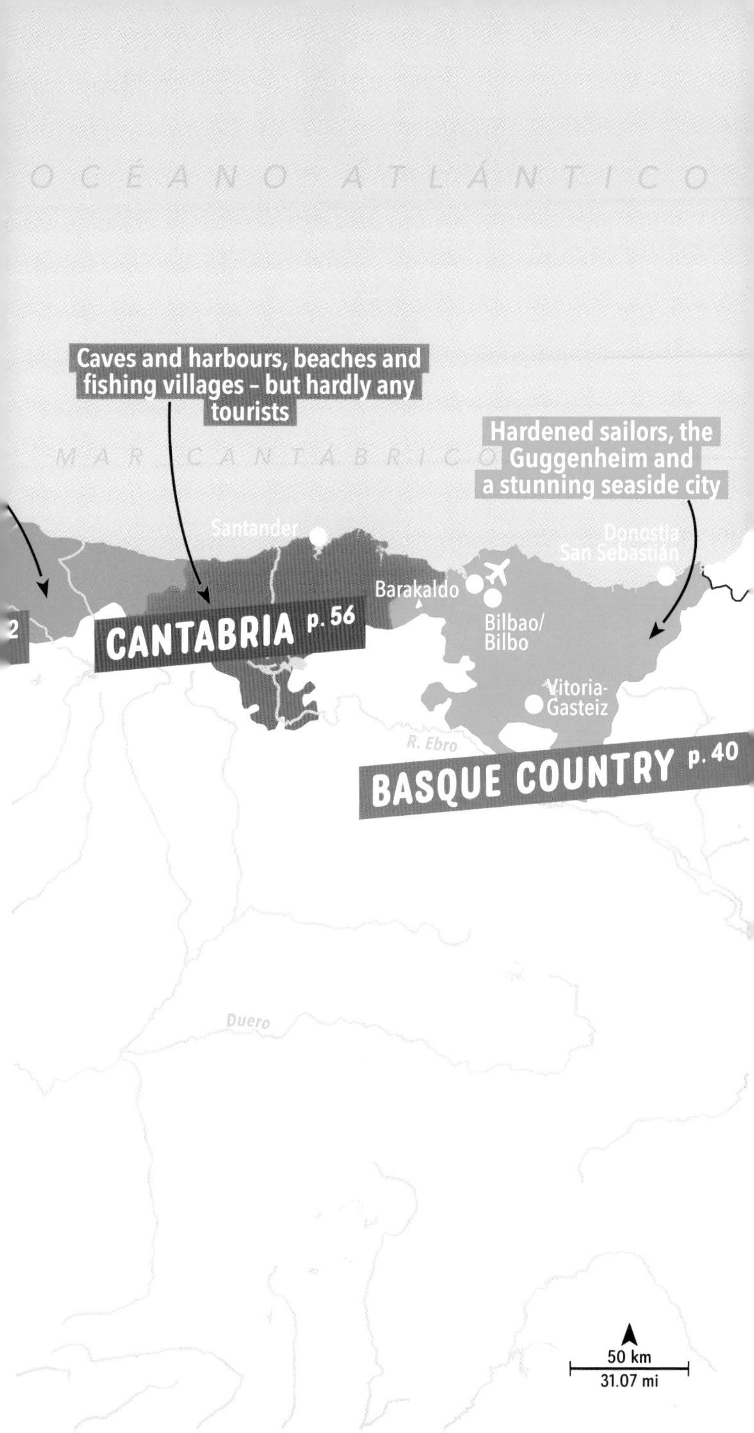

OCÉANO ATLÁNTICO

MAR CANTÁBRICO

Caves and harbours, beaches and fishing villages – but hardly any tourists

Hardened sailors, the Guggenheim and a stunning seaside city

Santander

Donostia
San Sebastián

Barakaldo

2

Bilbao/
Bilbo

CANTABRIA p. 56

Vitoria-
Gasteiz

R. Ebro

BASQUE COUNTRY p. 40

Duero

50 km
31.07 mi

BASQUE COUNTRY

NAUTICAL CHARM & BELLE ÉPOQUE

It wasn't so long ago that tourists gave the Basque Country a wide berth. But things have changed since then. The opening of the Guggenheim Museum in Bilbao, which transformed the city from a grimy industrial centre to a trendy holiday hotspot, was partly responsible for this shift in attitudes. Nowadays, fishing villages attract foodies and surfers with their abundant fish stocks and wild, untouched beaches. They also attract fans of the cult series *Game of Thrones*, but more on that later.

La Concha bay in San Sebastián is hard to beat

Bilbao's long-time rival San Sebastián, one of the most beautiful cities in Europe with one of the most stunning city beaches in the world, boasts multiple Michelin-starred restaurants and countless excellent *pintxo* bars.

BASQUE COUNTRY

San Juan de Gaztelugatxe ★ 9
Armintza
Bakio 8
Playa de Mundaka
Bermeo 10
Mundaka 11
Playa de Laga ★
Playa de Laida
Barrika Plentzia
Lemoiz
Urdaibai Nature Reserve ★ 12
Ibarrangelu
Sopela Urduliz Maruri-Jatabe
Berango
Getxo Elexalde Mungia
Arrieta
Ereño
Lekeitio ★ 14
Murueta
Kortezubi
Gizaburuaga
Fruiz
7 Puente de Vizcaya ★
Erandio
Morga
Aulesti
Gamiz - Fika
Derio
Muxika 15 Gernika
Museo Guggenheim ★
Mendata
Barakaldo
Larrabetzu
Munitibar-
Arbatzegi-Gerrikaitz
Ziortza-
Bolibar
Bilbao ★
p. 50
Etxebarri N637
EUSKADI
Alonsotegi
Basauri Galdakao
Amorebieta-
Etxano
Arrigorriaga
Lemoa
Ermua
Zaldibar
Arrankudiaga
Ugao-Miraballes
Igorre
Durango
AP68
Okondo Zeberio
Mañaria
Laudio/
Llodio
Artea Atxondo
N636
Areatza
Orozko
100km, 1 hr 15 mins
Luiaondo
AP68
N240
Amurrio
Ibarra

MARCO POLO HIGHLIGHTS

★ **SAN SEBASTIÁN**
Elegant and packed to the brim with fabulous eating options ➤ p. 44

★ **PLAYA DE LA CONCHA**
San Sebastián's shell-shaped beach is one of the most beautiful city beaches in the world ➤ p. 47

★ **CHILLIDA LEKU**
Incredible open-air museum with works by the famous Basque artist ➤ p. 48

★ **BILBAO**
From black sheep to tourist hotspot, thanks to the "Guggenheim effect" ➤ p. 50

★ **MUSEO GUGGENHEIM**
No trip to Bilbao would be complete without a visit to Frank Gehry's fish-like art gallery ➤ p. 50

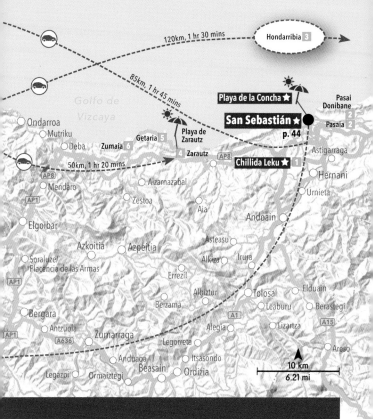

★ **PUENTE DE VIZCAYA**
Cross the Nervión via the oldest ferry bridge in the world ➤ p. 53

★ **SAN JUAN DE GAZTELUGATXE**
Head up 241 steps to the seafarers' chapel that has gained cult status since it featured in *Game of Thrones* ➤ p. 54

★ **URDAIBAI NATURE RESERVE**
This UNESCO biosphere reserve is a favourite destination for more than just birds and birders ➤ p. 54

★ **PLAYA DE LAGA**
One of the wildest, most beautiful beaches in the Basque Country ➤ p. 55

★ **LEKEITIO**
True fishing village vibes, complete with lighthouse ➤ p. 55

SAN SEBASTIÁN

(□ Q3) Is ★ San Sebastián, known as Donostia in the Basque language, the most beautiful city in the world? The 188,000 proud residents of the chic seaside resort, where Queen Isabel II sought a cure for her herpes in the mid-19th century and which the monarch María Cristina chose as her summer residence in 1887, believe that it is.

With its three beaches, including the famous *Concha*, three mountains, a historic old town with countless *pintxo* bars, several Michelin-starred restaurants, a charming harbour and chic new town from the early 20th century, aptly named the *Área Romántica*, the capital of the province of Guipúzcoa is an absolute gem.

SIGHTSEEING

AQUARIUM 🛝 🎡

The must-see attraction is the glass tunnel through the oceanarium containing two million litres of water, in which you can see sharks, moray eels and other unearthly creatures. Of course, there are also additional tanks with local and exotic marine wildlife. *April–June, Sept Mon–Fri 10am–7pm, Sat/Sun 10am–8pm, July/Aug 10am–8pm daily, Oct–March Tue–Sun 11am–7pm | 14 euros, children 7 euros | Plaza Carlos Blasco de Imaz 1 | aquariumss.com | ⏱ 2 hrs*

WHERE TO START?

At **La Concha**, of course! The famous shell-shaped beach is the ideal place to drink in San Sebastián's legendary beauty and a handy starting point to discover the port and the old town. The city centre – where you can also find the train station and bus station – is easy to get around on foot.

MONTE IGUELDO

The *funicular*, built in 1912, takes you up the city's mountain. At the top, there is a spectacular view over the bay and an 🎡 *amusement park (monteigueldo.es)* for children, with a roller coaster that takes you along the side of a sheer drop.

MONTE URGULL

You can climb on foot to the summit of Monte Urgull, which features a statue of Jesus reminiscent of the one in Rio de Janeiro. Here, you will stumble upon the remains of the *Castillo de la Mota* (now a history museum). The more melancholic among you should stop off at the *Cementerio de los Ingleses*, containing the derelict graves of soldiers killed in the Carlist Wars.

> **INSIDER TIP**
> Enchanting, romantic atmosphere

MUSEO MARÍTIMO VASCO 🐟

The lovingly designed maritime museum in its 18th-century building houses temporary exhibitions on the history of the Basque people and the

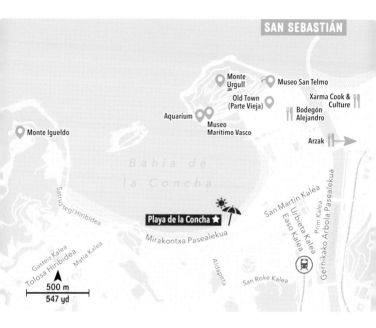

SAN SEBASTIÁN

Monte Urgull
Museo San Telmo
Old Town (Parte Vieja)
Xarma Cook & Culture
Aquarium
Bodegón Alejandro
Museo Maritimo Vasco
Monte Igueldo
Arzak

Bahía de la Concha

Playa de la Concha ★

Satrustegi Hiribidea
Mirakontxa Pasealekua
San Martin Kalea
Urbieta Kalea
Easo Kalea
Prim Kalea
Gernikako Arbola Pasealekua

Gasteiz Kalea
Tolosa Hiribidea
Matia Kalea
Aldapeta
San Roke Kalea

500 m
547 yd

sea. *Tue–Sat 10am–2pm and 4–7pm, Sun 11am–2pm, mid-June–mid-Sept also 4–7pm | free admission | Paseo del Muelle 24 | itsasmuseoa.eus | ⏱ 1 hr*

MUSEO SAN TELMO

The museum, housed in a modern extension to a 16th-century Dominican monastery, displays artworks from various eras and temporary exhibitions, as well as depicting Basque history and society from its inception until the end of the Franco dictatorship in the 1970s, using a multimedia approach and a carefully curated atmosphere. *Tue–Sun 10am–7pm, April–Oct 10am–8pm | 6 euros, ☞ Tue free | Plaza de Zuloaga | santelmomuseoa.eus | ⏱ 1½ hrs*

OLD TOWN (PARTE VIEJA)

The *Plaza de la Constitución* at the heart of the old town was once used as a bullring, evidenced by the numbers above the balconies of the surrounding houses. In the neighbouring side streets, the tables of the bars groan under the weight of myriad *pintxo* delicacies. Above the entrance to the 1774 *Basílica de Santa María* in Calle Mayor, the city's rather attractive namesake watches over his flock.

EATING & DRINKING

ARZAK

Juan Mari Arzak (now together with his daughter Elena) is considered one of Spain's finest chefs. Long-time holder of three Michelin stars, with the popularity and price tag to match.

Be sure to reserve (several weeks) in advance! *Sun/Mon closed | Av. Alcalde José Elósegui 273 | tel. 9 43 27 84 65 | arzak.es | €€€*

BODEGÓN ALEJANDRO

An inexpensive place for anyone who wants to taste sophisticated Basque cuisine at affordable prices. *Wed/Thu closed | C/ Fermín Calbetón 4 | tel. 9 43 42 71 58 | bodegonalejandro.com | €€*

PINTXO BARS

A traditional *txikiteo* will take you from bar to bar trying *pintxos* along with a glass of wine (the *txikito*). Here is a selection of the best: *148 Gastroleku (C/ Iñigo 1 | 148gastroleku.com)* with its incredible tartar; *Ganbara (C/ San Jerónimo 21 | ganbarajatetxea.com)* with its legendary mushroom dishes; *Gandarias (C/ 31 de Agosto 23 | restaurantegandarias.com)* with its superb *chuletas*; *La Viña (C/ 31 de Agosto 3 | lavinarestaurante.com)* with the best cheesecake of all time; *Néstor (C/ Pescadería 11 | bar-nestor.negocio. site)* with its heavenly tomato salad; *Paco Bueno (C/ Mayor 6)* with its succulent *gambas*; *Bar Txepetxa (C/ Pescadería 5 | bartxepetxa.es)* with fantastic spider crabs *(centollos).*

XARMA COOK & CULTURE

A cool restaurant with a tattooed chef in the surfing neighbourhood of Gros. Young Basque cuisine with fusion elements. *Tue closed | C/ Miguel Imaz 1 | tel. 9 43 14 22 67 | xarmacook.com | €€*

Pintxos made from local porcini mushrooms are highly prized at Ganbara

SHOPPING

The new town is a shopper's paradise filled with fashionable boutiques. The Gros neighbourhood is home to row upon row of surfing shops. You can buy traditional head coverings at *Leclercq (C/ Narrica 18 und C/ Fermín Calbetón 30 | sombrererialeclercq. com)*. *Alboka (Plaza Constitución 8 | albokaartesania.com)* is a treasure trove of Basque souvenirs. And if you aren't fed up with the *xirimiri* (drizzle), *Perfumería Benegas (C/ Garibay 12)* has created the fragrance "SSirimiri", which captures its scent perfectly.

SPORT & ACTIVITIES

The main mode of transport in San Sebastián is the bicycle. You can hire one at places such as *Bici Rent Donosti (Av. Zurriola 22 | tel. 9 43 27 11 73 | bicirentdonosti.es)*. Joggers love the *Paseo Nuevo* along the seafront, where a fresh breeze always blows. The walk above the coast on *Monte Ulía* to the port of Pasaia offers incredible views. You can rent surfboards and book surf lessons at Zurriola Beach, using companies like *Zurriola Surf Eskola (C/ Usandizaga 14 | tel. 9 43 01 13 91 | zurriolasurfeskola.com)*.

BEACHES

The ★ ⚲ *Playa de la Concha*, the shell-shaped beach with the nearby *Isla Santa Clara* and the elegant railings along the promenade, is one of the most beautiful city beaches in the world. A family-friendly option to the west of this is the *Playa de Ondarreta*, from where you can see Eduardo Chillida's sculpture *Peine del Viento* (Wind Comb), one of the city's famous landmarks. The wild breakers at *Playa Zurriola* make it a surfing hotspot. If you go for a walk along La Concha, make sure you slap the wall or the rocks at each end – otherwise you'll out yourself as a tourist!

INSIDER TIP
Stroll along the beach like a local

WELLNESS

LA PERLA

Spoil yourself at this wellness haven right on La Concha beach. Treatments such as thalassotherapy are available. *Core opening hours 8.30am–8.30pm daily | Paseo de la Concha | tel. 9 43 45 88 56 | la-perla.net*

NIGHTLIFE

When the sun sets, the streets of the old town throng with locals and tourists. For classical or jazz concerts, try the *Kursaal (Av. de Zurriola 1 | kursaal. eus)* and the *Teatro Victoria Eugenia (Paseo República Argentina 4 | victoria eugenia.eus)*. Check out some Basque rock and pop at *Le Bukowski (C/ Egia 18 | lebukowski.com)* and *Dabadaba (C/ Mundaiz 8 | dabadabass.com)*. *Bataplán (Paseo de la Concha | bataplandisco.com)* is *the* place to be for young people. For a jazzy, soulful atmosphere, head to *¡Be Club! (Paseo de Salamanca 3 | beclubss.com)* or *Altxerri (C/ Reina Regente 2 | altxerri jazzbar.com)* round the corner.

AROUND SAN SEBASTIÁN

1 CHILLIDA LEKU ★

7km south of San Sebastián/20 mins by bus BU 05 from the town centre

One of the Basque Country's main attractions is a traditional 16th-century *caserío* (farmhouse), which was restored by the famous Basque sculptor Eduardo Chillida (1924–2002). Chillida's sculptures can be found the world over, from the World Bank headquarters in Washington to the German Chancellery building in Berlin. Now a museum, the farmhouse has many drawings and engravings on display. Most spectacular of all are the extensive grounds of the house, which feature more than 40 of the artist's enormous iron and granite sculptures. *Opening times: see website | 12 euros | Hernani | Barrio Jáuregui 66 | museochillidaleku.com | ⏱ 2–3 hrs | ▦ Q4*

2 PASAIA & PASAI DONIBANE

5km east of San Sebastián/15 mins by bus E 09 from C/ Okendo

Take a walk through San Sebastián's industrial port *Pasaia* to the impressive shipyard of *Albaola (Tue–Sun 10am–2pm, Wed–Sat also 3–6pm, mid-May–mid-Sept until 7pm | 7 euros | albaola.org)*, where a replica whaling ship from the 16th century is being constructed. Afterwards, you can take the ferry (just 1.10 euros) to the medieval fishing village of *Pasai Donibane*, which is pretty much just a single street. *▦ R3*

3 HONDARRIBIA

22km east of San Sebastián/25 mins via the GI 636

The Basque Country's most beautiful medieval fishing town (17,000 inhabitants, Spanish: Fuenterrabía) is the preferred holiday destination for many Spanish city dwellers. You can walk along the river and beach promenades or explore the historical old town. *Pintxos* and *txakoli* abound in the fishing neighbourhood of *La Marina* with its colourfully painted cottages. For dinner, check out the Michelin-starred *Alameda (closed Mon/Tue and Sun evening | C/ Minasoroeta 1 | tel. 9 43 64 27 89 | restaurantealameda.net | €€€)*. For something cheaper, more down-to-earth and just as delicious, try local favourite *Arraunlari Berri (closed Tue | Paseo Butrón 3 | tel. 9 43 57 85 19 | arraunlariberri.com | €–€€). ▦ R3*

4 ZARAUTZ

21km west of San Sebastián/30 mins on the motorway

The 2.5km 🏖 beach at this popular seaside resort and surfing hotspot (23,000 inhabitants) that stretches along the Malecón promenade is the longest in the Basque Country. On the easternmost edge, there is a beautiful boardwalk that runs through the dunes. The town also boasts a lovely historic district and the *Conjunto Arqueológico Monumental Santa María La Real (staggered opening times, see website | 2 euros | menosca. com | ⏱ 1 hr)*, an attraction that includes a church, a medieval tower house and the art and history museum.

INSIDER TIP

Tasty fish stew

You can find the best *marmitako* served by Marian and Félix at *Euskalduna (daily | C/ Nagusia 37 | tel. 9 43 13 03 73 | FB | €).* ⊞ Q4

5 GETARIA

25km west of San Sebastián/40 mins via Zarautz

Getaria (2,800 inhabitants), with its striking mouse rocks, is primarily known as the birthplace of Juan Sebastián Elcano (1486–1526), the first man to circumnavigate the globe. Another famous Getaria native is fashion designer Cristóbal Balenciaga (1895–1972), who has a dedicated museum here, the fashionable *Cristóbal Balenciaga Museoa (Nov– March Tue–Sun 11am–3pm, April– June, Sept/Oct 11am–7pm, July/Aug daily 11am–8pm | 10 euros | Parque Aldamar 6 | cristobalbalenciaga museoa.com |* ⊙ *1½ hrs)*, which is worth a visit whether you're a hard-core fashionista or not. If you're not into couture, have a wander round *San Salvador* church with its wonky floor. Don't believe us? Go in and see! You can also drink local *txakoli*, eat *rodaballo* (turbot) or *besugo* (sea bream), at venues including gourmet restaurant *Elkano (closed Tue and every evening except Fri/Sat | C/ Herrerieta 2 | tel. 9 43 14 00 24 | res- tauranteelkano.com | €€€).* ⊞ Q3-4

6 ZUMAIA

35km west of San Sebastián/40 mins on the motorway

Zumaia (10,000 inhabitants), together with the neighbouring towns of Deba and Mutriku, make up the *Basque*

Sculptures by Basque artist Eduardo Chillida are displayed in the grounds of Chillida Leku

Coast Geopark, which boasts unique rock formations: the flysch. The *Algorri (June–Sept Tue–Sun 10am–2pm and 3–6pm, March–May Tue–Sun, Oct–Feb Thu–Sun 10am–1.30pm | C/ Juan Belmonte 21 | algorri.eus)* information centre will tell you how to "read" the layers of rock like a book, and at the *Ruta del Flysch (reservations: tel. 9 43 14 33 96 | geoparkea.eus)* you can explore it by boat.

Film lovers should head to the beautiful chapel above the Playa de Itzurun, which was used in the wedding scene from cult comedy *Spanish Affair*. And the wild, romantic look of the flysch formations on Itzurun beach was the perfect fantasy setting to catch the eye of the location scouts for *Game of Thrones*, the seventh season of which was partly filmed here! 🚩 *Q4*

BILBAO

(🚩 P4) **It's hard to believe that ★ Bilbao (350,000 inhabitants), or Bilbo in the Basque language), was once an ugly industrial juggernaut.** The ascent of Vizcaya's capital city to tourist hotspot status is thanks to the Guggenheim effect, which began when the museum opened in 1997. Since then, tourists have flocked to the city in droves to visit the 700-year-old historical neighbourhood of *Casco Viejo* right by the Guggenheim, the attractive new town (Spanish: *Ensanche*) and the miles of waterside promenades along the Nervión river.

AZKUNA ZENTROA 👕

Designer Philippe Starck didn't hold back on this Art Nouveau building when creating the stylish leisure and cultural centre. The most eye-catching things are the 43 stelae in the main hall. The exhibitionists among you should bring a swimming costume. The glass bottom of the swimming pool allows people on the floor below to watch you swim around up above *(Mon–Fri 7am–10pm, Sat/Sun 9am–9pm | 7.05 euros). Plaza Arriquibar 4 | azkunazentroa.eus*

INSIDER TIP
Public viewing at the pool

MUSEO DE BELLAS ARTES

Bilbao's Museum of Fine Arts is currently undergoing extension work by architects Foster + Partners, and will be a building site until at least the end of 2024. Until then, you can visit exhibitions displaying 100 works from the collection, which rotate weekly – the current programme is on the website. *Mon and Wed–Sat 10am–8pm, Sun 10am–3pm | 🐦 Admission free during renovation work | Plaza del Museo 2 | museobilbao.com*

MUSEO GUGGENHEIM ★

Almost more famous than the scale-covered museum designed by Frank Gehry are the two sculptures outside: *Puppy*, a giant, flower-covered puppy sculpture by Jeff Koons, and the terrifying spider *Maman* by Louise Bourgeois. Both of these, as well as several other artworks, can be viewed

for free 🐑 outside the museum itself. If you fancy paying the admission fee, check out the temporary exhibitions as well as the huge steel sculptures by Richard Serra. *Tue–Sun, mid-Jun–mid-Sept daily 10am–8pm | 15 euros, online 13 euros | Av. Abandoibarra 2 | guggenheim-bilbao.eus |* ⊙ *1½ hrs.*

MUSEO MARÍTIMO RÍA DE BILBAO

🐑 Outside the Maritime Museum, which is located on the site of a former shipyard, you can take a look at the old boats in the docks and a red loading crane that the *Bilbaínos* lovingly refer to as *Carola.* The museum itself vividly depicts the history of the Ría de Bilbao – sometimes using Playmobil figures. *April–Oct Tue–Sun 10am–8pm, Nov–March Tue–Sun 11am–7pm | 6 euros,* 🐑 *free Tue except July/Aug | Muelle*

Ramón de la Sota 1 | itsas museum.eus | ⊙ *1 hr*

MUSEO VASCO

This museum is located in a 17th-century Jesuit college and displays

WHERE TO START?

The **Guggenheim**, of course! The closest places to park are Plaza Euskadi and Plaza Pío Baroja. If you're arriving by bus, take the metro right by the bus station from San Mamés to Moyúa station and from there you can walk to Alameda Recalde and the Guggenheim. After visiting the museum, take a walk along the river to the old town.

Bilbao's Old Town, *Casco Viejo*

pieces relating to all aspects of Basque history: from prehistoric funerary monuments and whale hunting tools to ironmongery and pots. *Planned closure until end of 2024 due to renovation work | Plaza Miguel Unamuno 4 | euskalmuseoa.eus*

OLD TOWN (CASCO VIEJO)

The 700-year-old historic city centre with its long-established shops nestling beside trendy bars and pubs is known to the locals as *Siete Calles*, Seven Streets, but there is actually a lot more to it than that. At the heart of the neighbourhood is the 19th-century *Plaza Nueva* surrounded by ornate arcades.

EATING & DRINKING

CAFÉ BAR BILBAO

Since 1911, this traditional pub in the old town has been one of the most popular watering holes for *Bilbaínos*. *Daily | Plaza Nueva 6 | tel. 9 44 15 16 71 | bilbao-cafebar.com | €*

CAFÉ IRUÑA

Opened in 1903, this café with its neo-Moorish decor is the most beautiful and best known in the city. Order the *Aqua de Bilbao* and let yourself be surprised! *Daily | Colón de Larreátegui 13 | tel. 9 44 23 70 21 | cafeirunabilbao.net | €-€€*

INSIDER TIP
What do the Bilbaínos call "water"?

LA VIÑA DEL ENSANCHE

A rustic traditional restaurant which is constantly full of locals. Their ham is amazing! *Closed Sun | C/ Diputación 10 | tel. 9 44 15 56 15 | lavinadel ensanche.com | € €€*

MARKINA

The finest Basque cuisine with no frills. The *Bilbaínos* love their succulent steaks and fresh grilled fish. *Daily | C/ Henao 31 | tel. 9 44 23 25 40 | restaurantemarkina.com | €-€€*

SHOPPING

For stylish brands and boutiques, check out the *Gran Vía de Don Diego López de Haro* in the new town. For local specialities, try the 🛆 *Mercado de la Ribera (Mon 8am–2.30pm, Tue–Fri 8am–2.30pm and 5–8pm, Sat 8am–*

3pm | C/ de la Ribera), an Art Deco covered market on the banks of the Nervión dating back to 1929. If you have a sweet tooth, check out confectioners *Martina de Zuricalday (martinazuricalday.com)*, with several shops, who have been manufacturing irresistible sweet treats since 1830.

SPORT & ACTIVITIES

The riverside promenades along the Nervión are the perfect stomping ground for joggers, skaters and cyclists alike. Bikes can be hired from *Urban Bike (FEVE-Bahnhof Concordia | C/ Bailén 2 | tel. 9 44 07 73 73)* and *Tourné Bilbao (C/ Villarías 1 | tel. 9 44 24 94 65 | tournebilbao.com)*. For boat tours through Bilbao or to the ocean, contact *Bilboats (Pantalán Pío Baroja | tel. 9 46 42 41 57 | bilboats.com)*.

NIGHTLIFE

In the new town, *Calle Ledesma*, Bilbao's food and nightlife hotspot, is the place to be. And you can let your hair down in the old town too, at places like the cocktail bar *Patente #5974 (C/ Henao 6)*. If you fancy rocking out, head to *Grafit (C/ Urrutia 1)* or *Singular (C/ Lersundi 2)*. For live Basque music, try *Kafe Antzokia (C/ San Vicente 2)* or *Cotton Club (C/ Gregorio de la Revilla 25)*. For something really heavy, check out *Bilbo Rock (Muelle de la Merced 1)*: this converted church has become something of a cult venue. A newcomer to the city is *Sala Moma (C/ Rodríguez Arias 66)* which hosts concerts and exclusive

parties. *Euskalduna (Av. Abandoibarra 4 | euskalduna.eus)* is a concert hall where classical music is performed. A magnificent venue where you can watch concerts, comedy and ballet is the *Teatro Arriaga (Plaza Arriaga 1 | teatroarriaga.eus)*, dating back to 1890.

AROUND BILBAO

7 PUENTE DE VIZCAYA ★
13km northwest of Bilbao/18 mins via metro line L1 from Moyúa to Areeta
The oldest ferry bridge in the world, which is protected by UNESCO World Heritage status, has been shipping passengers from the town of Portugalete across the Nervión to Getxo since 1893. If you're not afraid of heights, you can cross the *pasarela* on foot at a height of 50m above the water instead of in the gondola at ground level. *Lift open daily 10am–2pm and 4–8pm | lift and pasarela 9.50 euros, pedestrian crossing in the gondola 0.50 euros | puente-colgante.com |* ⊞ O3

8 BAKIO
30km north of Bilbao/35 mins via the BI 631 and BI 2101
This holiday resort (2,700 inhabitants) has a beautiful beach stretching almost 1km. Fancy a tipple? Why not try the *Txakolingunea (May/June and Sept/Oct Mon–Sat 10am–2pm and 4–6pm, Sun 10am–3pm; July/Aug*

daily 10am–3pm and 4–7pm; Nov–April Tue–Sun 10am–2pm | 3.50 euros | Basigoko Bide Nagusia 3). Here you can learn about the history and production of the ⚑ Basque white wine Txakoli and knock back a couple of sample glasses while you're at it. ⚐ *P3*

9 SAN JUAN DE GAZTELUGATXE ★

35km north of Bilbao/45 mins via Bakio

A 2km walk and 241 steps will certainly leave you out of breath, but it's worth it. This fairytale seafarers' chapel dates back almost 1,000 years, with the latest iteration having been built in 1886 from the remains of its destroyed predecessors. San Juan de Gaztelugatxe has always been a tourist hotspot, but since parts of the seventh season of *Game of Thrones* were filmed there, the tiny island has cemented its cult status. Dragonstone Castle itself may have been an elaborate CGI creation, but the stairs are real as can be. ⚐ *P3*

10 BERMEO

35km northeast of Bilbao/40 mins via the BI 631

Long ago, this port (17,000 inhabitants) served as the capital of Vizcaya (1476–1602); today it is a typical rough-and-ready fishing backwater: hardy blokes pace the streets, old seamen prop up the bar in the pubs on the quay, and tourists are few and far between. If you're feeling fit, you can make the steep climb to the old town. In the medieval *Casa Torre de Ertzilla*

you will find the interactive fishing museum *Museo del Pescador (April–Sept Tue–Sat 10am–2pm and 4–7pm, Sun 10am–2pm; Oct–March Tue–Sat 10am–4pm, Sun 10.30am–2.30pm | 3.50 euros).* Make sure you take a boat tour (booking essential) from Bermeo to Urdaibai Biosphere Reserve: *Hegaluze | tel. 6 66 79 10 21 | hegaluze.com |* ⚐ *P3*

11 MUNDAKA

40km northeast of Bilbao/45 mins via Bermeo

A lovely little tourist spot with a harbour, a 🏖 beach and a picturesque chapel on a cliff? That's what Mundaka (1,850 inhabitants) looks like at first glance. In reality, it's an internationally renowned surfer's paradise, home to the "lefthander", the most famous left-breaking wave in Europe. It doesn't come often, but when it does it can reach 4m high and 400m wide. The perfect challenge for advanced surfers! ⚐ *P3*

12 URDAIBAI NATURE RESERVE ★

40km to the Urdaibai Bird Center northeast of Bilbao/50 mins via the motorway to Amorebieta and the BI 635 and BI 2238

The swampy estuary of the Río Oka has been declared a UNESCO Biosphere Reserve thanks to its beauty and biodiversity. Visit the 🦉 *Urdaibai Bird Center (staggered opening times, see website | 7 euros, children 4 euros | Orueta Auzoa 7 | birdcenter.org |* 🕐 *1–2 hrs)* to discover the area and its inhabitants. ⚐ *P3*

🔟 PLAYA DE LAIDA & PLAYA DE LAGA

45km north of Bilbao /55 mins via the motorway to Amorebieta and the BI 635 and BI 2238

Nestled among the dunes, the 🐾 *Playa de Laida*, which extends for almost 1km, is the longest beach on the Ría de Mundaka, and the water is shallow, making it a great place for families. Just 2km away, you will find the ★ 🐾 *Playa de Laga*, which is almost 600m long and is one of the wildest, most beautiful beaches in the Basque Country. A surfer's paradise! *P3*

🔟 LEKEITIO ★

55km northeast of Bilbao/1 hr via the motorway to Amorebieta and the BI 635 and BI 2238

The prettiest fishing village in Vizcaya (7,200 inhabitants), with the *Playa Karraspio* and *Playa Isuntza* beaches, has everything you need for a relaxing time. Your first port of call should be the information centre at the *Faro de Santa Catalina*, where you can take a virtual boat trip *(Sat/Sun, July/Aug Wed–Sun, with guide only, book in advance!|6 euros|tel. 9 46 84 40 17| lekeitioturismo.eus)*. Slow right down with a stop on one of the terraces of the harbour by the historic fishing quarter and enjoy the view of the uninhabited island of Garraitz. It's so picturesque you'll think it was put there on purpose by the tourism board! Then you can try some freshly caught seafood at places like *Mesón Arropain (closed Sun evening and Mon–Thu except July/Aug | Iñigo*

Artieta Etorbidea 5|tel. 9 46 24 31 83| FB | €€). P3

🔟 GERNIKA (GUERNICA)

35km east of Bilbao/40 mins via the AP 8 and BI 635

The town (17,000 inhabitants) drew international attention due to a devastating bomb attack by the German Condor Legion during the Spanish Civil War in 1937, which Pablo Picasso immortalised in his painting of the same name. The 🐦 *Casa de Juntas (daily 10am–2pm and 4–6pm, mid-June–mid-Sept until 7pm | free admission | Allende Salazar 1 | jjgg bizkaia.net)*, the magnificent parliament building from 1833, is an incredible sight, with its ancient oak in the garden which is sacred to the Basque people, symbolising freedom and independence – hence the bombing in 1937. *P3-4*

Bermeo harbour

CANTABRIA

CAVES, SEA & SANTANDER

Cantabria is probably the most "Spanish" region in Northern Spain. While there is a regional language called *cántabro*, hardly anyone can speak it. Instead, they use highly formal Castilian Spanish (a concept that is wholly alien in the Basque Country).

Cantabria's 220km of coastline boast countless beaches, primarily frequented by Spanish tourists with holiday homes here. This means that some bathing spots have a rather mournful air in the off season,

Centro Botín in Santander is an art complex with an ocean view

especially places like Laredo, with its 5km *playa* of the same name. Even historic towns such as Castro Urdiales in the east and San Vicente de la Barquera in the west are rather quiet outside the tourist season. The exception is the Cueva de Altamira, whose rock paintings are among the most famous in the world.

The highlight of the region is Santander, an elegant, reserved beauty with chic bathing areas and a marina. Here, you can experience Spanish grandeur without other tourists getting in your way.

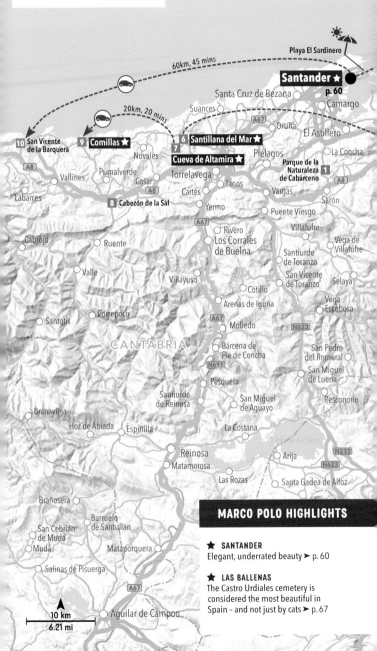

CANTABRIA

Playa El Sardinero

60km, 45 mins

Santander ★
p. 60

Santa Cruz de Bezana

Camargo

Suances

Oruña

El Astillero

20km, 20 mins

A67

10 San Vicente de la Barquera

9 **Comillas** ★

Novales

6 **Santillana del Mar** ★

7 **Cueva de Altamira** ★

Piélagos

La Concha

Parque de la Naturaleza de Cabárceno **1**

A8

A8

Vallines

Pumalverde

Casar

Torrelavega

Tanos

Vargas

Sarón

A8

Labarces

Cartes

Yermo

Puente Viesgo

A67

8 Cabezón de la Sal

Rivero

Villafufre

Vega de Villafufre

Cabrojo

Ruente

Los Corrales de Buelna

Santiurde de Toranzo

Valle

Villayuso

San Vicente de Toranzo

Selaya

Cotillo

Vega Escobosa

Santotís

Correpoco

Arenas de Iguña

A67

Molledo

N623

CANTABRIA

Bárcena de Pie de Concha

San Pedro del Romeral

N611

Pesquera

San Miguel de Luena

Branavieja

Santiurde de Reinosa

San Miguel de Aguayo

Resconorio

Hoz de Abiada

Espinilla

La Costana

Embalse del Ebro

Reinosa

Arija

N232

Matamorosa

N623

Brañosera

Las Rozas

Santa Gadea de Alfoz

Barruelo de Santullán

San Cebrián de Muda

Mataporquera

Muda

Salinas de Pisuerga

A67

10 km
6.21 mi

Aguilar de Campoo

MARCO POLO HIGHLIGHTS

★ **SANTANDER**
Elegant, underrated beauty ➤ p. 60

★ **LAS BALLENAS**
The Castro Urdiales cemetery is considered the most beautiful in Spain – and not just by cats ➤ p. 67

OCÉANO ATLÁNTICO
MAR CANTÁBRICO

70km, 50 mins

Ajo ○   Arnuero ○   ○ Noja
                          ☀
○ Carriazo   Playa de Berria
         Escalante ○ Santoña 2
Villaverde   ○ Beranga ○ Gama   ☀
de Pontones   ○ Cicero 3 Playa de Laredo
    A8   Laredo
   Entram-   4 Monte Candina   Las Ballenas ★
   basaguas ○ Solórzano   ○ Liendo   5 Castro Urdiales
70km, 50 mins
○ La Cavada   ○ Bádames ○ Limpias   Sámano ○   ○ Ontón
Barrio de Arriba   ○ Ampuero ○ El Puente   A8
                                                        Muskiz ○

                        ○ Rasines
Bustablado ○   Sierra Alcomba   ○ Alen   ○ Arenao
        ○ Riva   ○ Gibaja   Turtzioz ○
La Cárcoba ○   ○ Arredondo Ramales   ○ La Matanza   ○ Carral
           Val del Asón de la Victoria   Artzentales
○ La Pedrosa   Karrantza Harana /   Zalla ○
         ○ Lanestosa   Valle de Carranza
○ La Concha   EUSKADI   ○ Balmaseda
         ○ Veguilla
              N629

○ Las Machorras   ○ Artziniega

Espinosa de   ○ Villasana
los Monteros   de Mena
          ○ Villasante de Montija
                    ○ Castrobarto
○ Cornejo
CASTILLA Y LEÓN   ○ Quincoces de Yuso
          N629

SANTANDER

(□ N3) **There's a Playa de la Concha in ★ Santander too. The city is the main rival of the Basque Country's San Sebastián when it comes to their pasts as chic bathing hotspots.**

Santander tends to come off second best – but that might just be down to the fact that its had its fair share of tragedy. Cantabria's capital (173,000 inhabitants) really has been through the wars. In 1893, the dynamite on board the cargo ship *Cabo Machichaco* exploded, covering the port in debris and ash and killing almost 600 people. As if one disaster wasn't enough, strong winds caused a fire that broke out by the harbour in 1941 to spread to the historic old town, destroying the homes of thousands of people.

But Santander has a sunny side too: the city's beautiful Magdalena Peninsula sports what was once the

holiday residence of King Alfonso XIII and his consort Victoria Eugenia, whom the Spanish nobility followed in droves to summer resorts in the early 20th century. Other buildings from that time include the Palacio Real and the chic casino in the Belle Époque style on Sardinero beach. The city is also famed for lending its name to Santander bank, whose headquarters in the centre overshadow even the cathedral and royal palace.

WHERE TO START?

Drink in the sea breeze! **Paseo Pereda**, the central promenade, is a particularly good place to start. If you're arriving by car, your best bet is to head for Alfonso XIII Paseo Pereda or Machichaco car parks. You can easily walk into town from there. To get to Sardinero beach and the Magdalena Peninsula, you can rent a bike *(tusbic.es, estación Jardines de Pereda)* or go by bus, for example the no. 11 *(15 mins)*. Get off at Plaza Italia.

SIGHTSEEING

Please note: many city maps include several museums that aren't mentioned here. These are either only open a few days a year, have been undergoing renovations for years, or are permanently closed.

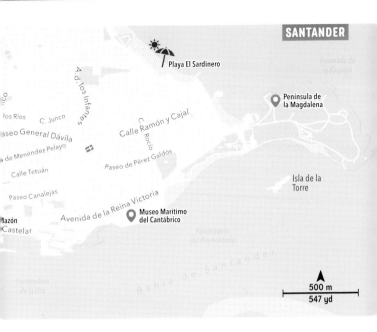

SANTANDER

Playa El Sardinero

A. d. los Infantes

los Ríos

C. Junco

Calle Ramón y Cajal

aseo General Dávila

de Menéndez Pelayo

C. Rocío

Calle Tetuán

Paseo de Pérez Galdós

Península de la Magdalena

Paseo Canalejas

Avenida de la Reina Victoria

lazón

Castelar

Museo Marítimo del Cantábrico

Isla de la Torre

Ensenada de la Raspua

Fondeadero del Promontorio

Bahía de Santander

Fondeadem de la Osa

500 m
547 yd

CATEDRAL DE NUESTRA SEÑORA DE LA ASUNCIÓN

The cathedral, which started its life in the 13th century, was badly damaged in the harbour explosion in 1893. No sooner had it been restored than the church was ravaged by fire in 1941, and it took until the 1950s for it to be returned to its former state. The 15th-century cloister is particularly striking, and the tomb of Santander-born literary scholar Marcelino Menéndez y Pelayo (1856–1912) is also worth seeing.

CENTRO BOTÍN

The cultural centre and museum of modern art looks rather like a pair of high-tech binoculars on stilts. The centre, designed by Renzo Piano, houses temporary exhibitions, but the most impressive thing about it is the sea view. Artworks are positioned outside the entrance to attract visitors. *June – Sept Tue–Sun 10am–9pm; Oct–May Tue–Fri 10am–2pm and 4–8pm, Sat/Sun 10am–8pm | 9 euros | Muelle de Albareda, Jardines de Pereda | centrobotin.org | ⏱ 1–1½ hrs*

FUNICULAR DEL RÍO DE LA PILA 🐷

The free cable car – which is more of a glass lift than anything else – in the Calle Río de la Pila will gives you spectacular views over the city. *Daily 6am–midnight*

MUSEO MARÍTIMO DEL CANTÁBRICO

A modern museum with everything you could possibly want to know about the history of Cantabrian seafaring, the sea, and the things swimming around in it. The whale skeleton is particularly impressive, while the real-life giant squid is somewhat unnerving. *Tue–Sun 10am–6pm, May–Sept until 7.30pm | 8 euros | C/ Severiano Ballesteros | museosdecantabria.es |* ⏱ *1–1½ hrs*

MUSEO DE PREHISTORIA Y ARQUEOLOGÍA DE CANTABRIA (MUPAC)

The archaeological museum features ancient rocks, bones and everything else pre- and protohistoric Cantabria has to offer, presented via interactive multimedia. *Tue–Fri 10am–2pm and 5–7.30pm (May–Sept until 8pm), Sat/ Sun 10am–2pm and 5–8pm | 5 euros | Mercado del Este/C/ Bailén | museos decantabria.es |* ⏱ *1 hr*

PENÍNSULA DE LA MAGDALENA

The peninsula in the east of the city is one big leisure park. You can take the sightseeing train, sunbathe at Playa de los Bikinis (named after the foreign students who first demonstrated this type of swimwear here in the 1960s), admire the various sculptures scattered around and watch penguins and seals sunbathing in the 🐧 *Parque Marino*. When you see the replicas of three historic galleons, you will marvel at how Santander-born scientist Vital Alsar managed to cross the Atlantic Ocean. You can also visit the former summer residence of King Alfonso XIII and his consort Victoria Eugenia. The *Palacio Magdalena (opening times vary, see website | 6 euros | palacio magdalena.com)* now hosts summer courses from Menéndez Pelayo International University.

The sand at Playa El Sardinero is framed by the Magdalena peninsula

EATING & DRINKING

BODEGA LA CIGALEÑA
Rustic, traditional restaurant with plenty of wines on the menu. *Daily | C/ Daoíz y Velarde 19 | tel. 9 42 21 01 84 | cigalena.com | €€*

BODEGAS MAZÓN ⚑
This bar, which started life as a *bodega* in 1902, now serves regional cuisine. Among the traditional wine barrels are the locals, propping up the bar with a drink in hand. *Daily | C/ Hernán Cortés 57 | tel. 9 42 21 57 52 | bodegasmazon.com| €–€€*

CASA LITA
Bar recommended by Michelin with over 300 *pintxos* on the menu. *Closed Mon except July/Aug | Paseo Pereda 37 | tel. 9 42 36 48 30 | casalita.es | €–€€*

LA GRUTA DE JOSÉ
This cosy cave will make you feel as if you're at the bottom of the sea, all the while offering fresh and reasonably priced delicious Cantabrian fish dishes. *Closed Tue | C/ Gabildos 9 | tel. 9 42 13 47 18 | lagrutadejose.es | €€*

LA MAR OYSTERS & DRINKS
Stylish bar with cool atmosphere and even cooler patrons. The perfect place to try Cantabrian oysters! *Closed Sun evening | C/ Peña Herbosa 11 | tel. 6 27 72 73 84 | FB | €*

SHOPPING

The place to be when it comes to hopping in Santander is 🌂 *Mercado de la Esperanza*, which can be found in the plaza of the same name. This 1904 covered market sells everything edible Cantabria has to offer. The area around it also features extensive pedestrian zones and plenty of shopping streets.

SPORT & ACTIVITIES

For surfing and surfboard rental, check out the *Escuela de Surf Sardinero (Balneario 1a | escueladesurfsardinero. com)* or the *Escuela de Surf Santander (C/ Dr Marañón | escueladesurfsantander.com)* on the Playa Sardinero. The *Campo Municipal de Golf Mataleñas (Av. del Faro | golfmatalenas. com)* is considered one of the most beautiful courses in Spain thanks to its location by the sea. Or you can do as the locals do and go for a stroll: the most popular spots are the *Paseo* and the attached *Jardines de Pereda*.

BEACHES

Santander has plenty of beaches. The most famous and most popular among surfers and sun worshippers is the 🏄 *Playa El Sardinero* in the neighbourhood of the same name, with its casino and Belle Époque history. Right next to it is the *Playa de la Concha*, followed by the *Playa del Camello*, the *Playa de los Bikinis*, the *Playa de La Magdalena* on the peninsula, and, closest to the centre, the *Playa de los Peligros*. Furthest away and only reachable on foot, you also have the beautiful little *Playa Los Molinucos*.

NIGHTLIFE

In the evenings you will find young people partying in the *Calle Arrabal*. Seasoned clubbers swear by the *Sala Rocambole (C/ Hernán Cortés 35 | salarocambole.com)*. For a bit more sophistication and culture, check out the *Palacio de Festivales (C/ Gamazo | palaciofestivales.com)* with its wacky architecture.

> **INSIDER TIP**
> **Where's the party?**

For secret music, theatre and dance with an intimate ambience, head to the historic *El Principal (elprincipalteatro.com | tel. 6 06 89 79 50)*; bookings by phone only, and you will receive the address by text on the day of the performance.

AROUND SANTANDER

1 PARQUE DE LA NATURALEZA DE CABÁRCENO 👶

20km south of Santander/20 mins via the S 30 and CA 142

Is it a zoo or a nature reserve? Drive over 20km through the grounds in Obregón and watch animals from five continents in a gigantic enclosure, where their habitats in the wild have been recreated as faithfully as possible. Alternatively, you can ride in the cable car over the top! *March–Oct daily 9.30am–6pm; Nov–Feb Mon–Fri 9.30am–5pm, Sat/Sun 9.30am–6pm | 20–39 euros depending on the seasons, teens 10–21.50 euros, children*

6 euros | parquedecabarceno.com | ⏱ 3 hrs | 🗺 N3

2 SANTOÑA

45km east of Santander/40 mins via the A 8 and CA 241

In Santoña (1,050 inhabitants), it's all about cans – more specifically, the cans used to preserve *anchoas de Santoña*. This place sells the best anchovies in the whole of Spain, in shops like *Conservas Emilia (Av. de Carrero Blanco 25 | anchoasemilia.es)*. You'll pay through the nose, but these are delicacies after all.

Apart from that, the town is a strange cross between run-down fishing village and pretty port. Attractions include the church of *Santa María del Puerto* and the 17th-century *Fuerte de San Martín (at the time of writing the fort was closed to visitors until further notice | tourist information: tel. 9 42 66 00 66 | turismosantona.es)*, at the end of the sweeping Paseo Marítimo.

> **INSIDER TIP**
> **See the light(house)**

Around Monte Bucìero on the outskirts of town, there are several hiking routes up the mountain and to fortifications and lighthouses with incredible views (further information at *farodelcaballo.es*).

Immediately to the north of Santoña is one of the wildest beaches in Cantabria: the 🏖 *Playa de Berria*, which is almost 2km long, exudes a pioneer atmosphere – and is mostly deserted. Why is it so quiet here? It may be down to the walls and watchtowers of the Penal del Dueso prison on the eastern end of the beach. You

Cabo de Ajo is the most northerly point in Cantabria – and probably the windiest!

can find accommodation and surfing lessons with *Berria Surf School (berria surfschool.com)*.

Santoña's neighbouring towns of *Isla* and *Noja* have several beautiful beaches but not much else. A few miles behind Isla, you can find the *Cabo de Ajo*, where the lighthouse offers an incredible view of the coast. But be sure to bring a jacket to protect you from the stiff breeze!

The *Parque Natural de las Marismas de Santoña, Victoria y Joyel* nature reserve is a haven for our feathered friends, with around 120 species of bird paying a visit over the course of the year, including spoonbills and cormorants. There are viewpoints for watching the birds along the Río Asón estuary. Further information can be found at the 🐦 *Centro de Interpretación (opening times vary: check website near the time of your visit | admission free | farodelcaballo. es/centro-de-interpretacion-marismas-de-santona | ▥ N3)* at Santoña harbour. The locals are very proud of the modern concrete monstrosity that looks like a damaged ship's hull.

🛭 LAREDO

45km east of Santander/40 mins via the A 8

Apparently the "capital of the Costa Esmeralda" (11,200 inhabitants) experienced a tourism boom when Sergio Leone's sword-and-sandal film *The Colossus of Rhodes* hit the big screen in 1961. While the debut film of this cult director, who later became famous for his spaghetti westerns, garnered a mixed reception from critics, the beach and harbour in Laredo, where several scenes were filmed, blossomed into a tourist hotspot. In summer things really kick off on the 5km-long beach, but outside of high season there is hardly a soul in sight and the empty apartment blocks give off a slightly post-apocalyptic vibe.

Aside from its huge beach, Laredo also boasts a lovely historic centre with the Gothic church *Santa María de la Asunción*, though the atmosphere is somewhat spoiled by all the empty properties. The *tunnel* in Laredo is a rather eerie addition. Originally begun in the 19th century as a way of accessing the dock that was never finished, it served as a hideout for residents during the Spanish Civil War. Today, the tunnel is rather spooky and makes you feel as if you're running away from Jack the Ripper. But the lonely platform on the wild shore at the other end is worth the scary walk! ⌦ N–O3

INSIDER TIP
Feeling brave?

❹ MONTE CANDINA

55km east of Santander/45 mins via the A 8

The village of *Oriñón* (200 inhabitants, umpteen thousand in high season) has a beautiful beach but is otherwise just burger stands and cheap camping – nothing to write home about. It's still worth going there, or driving past it to *Sonabia* (another small village with a beautiful beach). From there, you get an incredible view of Monte Candina with a rock formation known as *Ojo del Diablo*. This "eye of the devil" is home to one of the coast's few vulture colonies. It's wonderful to watch the birds flying over the rocks and screeching as they go! ⌦ O3

INSIDER TIP
Circling vultures

❺ CASTRO URDIALES

70km east of Santander/50 mins via the A 8

The easternmost holiday resort in Cantabria (32,000 inhabitants) is apparently so popular among the neighbours that during the holidays there are more Basque people there than locals. And it's no wonder: the friendly town boasts two beaches (with five more in the surrounding area), a 1km-long promenade, elegant houses and palatial villas from the early 20th century. On the edge of the historic old town is the *Castillo de Santa Ana*, a quaint 12th- or 13th-century castle with a lighthouse (and exhibitions of work by artists of varying quality), which is right next to a medieval bridge with attached hermitage by the harbour. Add to this plenty of café and restaurant terraces and your charming tourist town is complete.

Of course, delicious seafood is regularly brought ashore at the docks. If you fancy a taste, we recommend *La Arboleda (closed Mon | C/ Ardigales 48 | tel. 9 42 87 19 93 | €€)* or *Asador El Puerto (daily | C/ Santa María | tel. 6 49 09 74 86 | asadorelpuerto.com | €€–€€€)*. The only slight oddity is that *Santa María de la Asunción* (whose construction began in the 13th century), which is considered the most noteworthy Gothic church in the whole of Cantabria, can't usually be visited in the morning because there is almost always a funeral taking place. Do more people die in Castro Urdiales

6 SANTILLANA DEL MAR ★
30km west of Santander/30 mins via the A 67 and CA 131

Jean-Paul Sartre described Santillana del Mar (4,200 inhabitants) as the "most beautiful village in Spain". And he wasn't lying, because the town,

Laredo is the understated capital of the Costa Esmeralda

than elsewhere? Who knows, but the deceased are certainly in luck: ★ *Las Ballenas*, the Neoclassical cemetery from 1893, is situated high up on a cliff above the town with fantastic views, and was designated the *Mejor Cementerio de España* (Best Cemetery in Spain) in 2017. This opinion is shared by the countless cats who live there and the locals, many of whom have built themselves unusual – and not always the most tasteful – resting places. 🕮 *03*

with its noble and bourgeois houses, churches and palaces dating from the 15th to the 17th century, has survived almost intact, right down to its paving stones. Although Sartre may have had a point, Santillana isn't exactly known for telling the truth. The name literally translates as "holy, flat and by the sea", although the place isn't holy, flat, or by the sea – which the locals themselves admit with a wink. This fib is what caused people to refer to it as the "Town of Three Lies".

The *cloister* of the 12th-century collegiate church *Colegiata de Santa Juliana* is well worth seeing. The church itself venerates the remains of the saint who gave the place its name. If you enjoy the frisson of fear, be sure to visit the torture museum: the *Museo de la Tortura (July–Sept daily 10am-9pm, Oct–June 10.30am-2pm and 3.30-7pm | 4 euros | C/ Bertrand Clisson 1 | museodelatortura.com)* displays various terror-inspiring ways people have used to torment one another throughout the centuries. Rather fittingly, it focuses primarily on the Spanish Inquisition. The 🦩 *zoo (daily 9.30am until sunset | 25 euros, children 10 euros | Av. del Zoo | zoo santillanadelmar.com)* in Santillana is considered one of the best in Spain. Entry costs an arm and a leg, but you'll get to see white tigers. 🚌 *M3*

7 CUEVA DE ALTAMIRA ★ ☂

35km southwest of Santander/ 35 mins via Santillana del Mar

In 1868, a tenant named Modesto Cubillas lost his hunting hound near Santillana del Mar. While searching for his runaway pooch, Cubillas stumbled across a cave and immediately informed the landowner, lawyer and hobby archaeologist Marcelino Sanz de Sautuola. In 1875, Sautuola visited the cave for the first time but didn't discover anything amazing about it. When visiting for the second time in 1879, the enthusiastic amateur scientist crawled on his hands and knees, looking for bones and tools on the ground. Luckily, his young daughter was with him that day. She could stand upright in the cave and was looking upwards when she suddenly shouted: "Look, Daddy! Cows!" So, it was in fact a small child who discovered what are probably the most famous rock paintings in the world. When her father made the discovery public, he was ridiculed in professional circles. The drawings were dismissed as "scribbles" and clumsy fakes, and by the time the scientific community realised its mistake and acknowledged Sautuola's contributions, he was no longer around to appreciate it. He died in 1888.

Altamira is now considered the "Sistine Chapel of rock art". The paintings, which are a designated UNESCO World Heritage Site, are between 15,000 and 22,000 years old, with one small painting coming in at a whopping 35,000 years old. The caves, with their colourful depictions of horses, goats, game and large numbers of bison, were closed to the public in 2002 because the visitors' breath was damaging the drawings so much that they were in danger of being destroyed. Today, you can visit a true-to-life replica of the cave, the *Neocueva (Tue–Sat 9.30am-6pm, May–Oct until 8pm, Sun 9.30am-3pm | 3 euros 🐂 Sat from 2pm and Sun unrestricted | C/ Marcelino Sanz de Sautuola | culturaydeporte.gob.es/mnaltamira | ⏱ 45 mins).* We highly recommend that you buy your ticket in advance during high season and at weekends, because the Neocueva also has limited tickets available.

Since 2015, the original cave has (not entirely uncontroversially) been open to five people per week. Every Friday between 9.30am and 10.30am, lots are drawn to decide which visitors will be allowed to enter. These are then admitted to the original cave at 10.40am for a strict 37 minute visit. 📖 M3

8 CABEZÓN DE LA SAL

*45km southwest of Santander/
35 mins via the A 67 and A 8*

This tiny town (8,500 inhabitants) with many well-preserved medieval buildings has a wonderfully relaxed atmosphere. Your best bet is to wander the streets early in the morning and watch as everything wakes up. You can find sustenance at the *Pastelería Las Hijas de Pedro (C/ Virgen del Campo | hojaldredecantabria.com)*, where the friendly baker Mariola will sell you the local delicacy *palucos de cabezón*, a sweet treat resembling a coconut macaroon. After you've wandered round the town, be sure to visit 🚩 *Poblado Cántabro (Wed–Sat 10am–2pm and 4–7pm, Sun 10am–2pm | 2 euros | regio cantabrorum.es)*, a reconstruction of an ancient village where you can have a nosy round the little houses and see just how "cosy" life was for Cantabrians 2,000 years ago. 📖 M4

Prehistoric bison in the Cueva de Altamira

Gaudí designed every inch of *El Capricho* – even the ridge tiles on the roof

🄈 COMILLAS ★

55km west of Santander/45 mins via the A 67, A 8 and CA 135

Comillas (2,200 inhabitants) is a rare gem. This is chiefly down to its many buildings in the *modernismo*, style, Spain's take on Art Nouveau. Some highlights are the former *Pontifical University* from 1883, the Gothic *cemetery* and the neo-Gothic, Modernist *Palacio de Sobrellano* (very staggered opening times, see website | 5 euros | *short.travel/nsk1*) from 1881, which looks like something straight out of a fantasy film. The tourist information centre has a good map with two routes on it: the *Ruta Monumental* that takes you to see the historical sights, and the *Ruta Modernista* that showcases the best examples of *modernismo*. You will also find a sizeable beach, a pretty harbour and a historic old town.

But the highlight is *El Capricho de Gaudí* (daily 10.30am–5.30pm; March–June and Oct until 8pm; July–Sept until 9pm | 7 euros | *Barrio de Sobrellano* | *elcaprichodegaudi.com* | ⏱ 1 hr), one of the first major buildings by the immensely imaginative Catalan architect. From 1883 to 1885, Gaudí, who was not yet 30, put together a mind-bending mishmash of bricks, tiles, wood, glass and wrought iron with towers, winding staircases, terraces and beautiful gardens. A bit mad, a bit muddled – but absolutely stunning. 🕮 M3

INSIDER TIP
Map your route – don't leave it to chance

🔟 SAN VICENTE DE LA BARQUERA

60km west of Santander/45 mins via the A 67 and A 8

This popular holiday resort (4,200 inhabitants) at the mouth of the Río del Escudo is one of the most beautiful coastal towns in Cantabria. The beaches and the town itself are connected via two bridges: the 15th-century *Puente de la Maza* which has no fewer than 28 arches, and the *Puente Nuevo* from the late 18th century.

Trudge your way up into the steep historic centre and you will find some beautiful 16th-century palaces next to the *Iglesia de Nuestra Señora de Los Ángeles*, built in a range of styles between the 8th and the 16th century. One quirky feature of the church is the Renaissance tomb of the priest Antonio del Corro who, instead of resting in peace, appears to be propped up on his elbow and reading as he awaits heaven. There is also a spectacular view from the *Castillo del Rey* of the Cantabrian mountains and the Picos de Europa, which loom up behind San Vicente like a gigantic wall. A narrow road leads past the lively fishing dock to the idyllically situated *Santuario de la Barquera*, which was built in the 15th century in honour of a somewhat alarming version of the Holy Virgin, who regularly appeared to sailors on board a ship without sails, oars or crew.

There are three beaches for that perfect holiday feeling: the *Playa de la Maza*, the *Playa Tostadero* and the *Playa de Merón*. If you finish your day at the beach looking like a lobster, you might feel an affinity with the area's local speciality, *arroz con bogavante* (rice with lobster). For a particularly delicious take on the dish, head to *Restaurante Augusto (daily | C/ Mercado 1 | tel. 9 42 71 20 40 | restauranteaugusto.es | €€)*.

Right next to San Vicente and situated in the *Parque Natural de Oyambre* is the 900m-long *Playa de Gerra*, which is popular among surfers thanks to its strong winds and impressive waves. Just a few hundred metres away is another surfing paradise, the *Playa de Oyambre*, which consists of almost 2km of beach surrounded by sand dunes. 🗺 *L–M3*

ASTURIAS

In 1969, some resourceful tourism experts had the idea of giving the Asturian coast on the Bay of Biscay the name Costa Verde. Indeed, the "Green Coast" is much greener than you would normally expect in Spain. In many spots, the lush meadows filled with plump grazing cows stretch as far as the beach.

Yet mass tourism is all but unknown here, and you don't need to wait in line to discover medieval gems like Oviedo or the less-pretty but all-the-more varied town of Gijón.

The "cider tree" in Gijón is a tribute to the region's favourite drink

The region is known for its *casas indianas*, named after the Asturians who emigrated to South America, came into money there, and returned home to erect these grand "Indian" palaces, which can be recognised both by their architecture and by their signature palm tree next to the door.

Asturias loves apple trees even more than it loves palm trees. Asturians are obsessed with the local cider, or *sidra*, which is knocked back in quantities at local *sidrerías*.

ASTURIAS

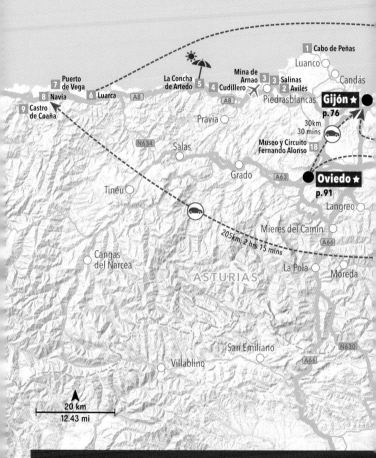

Cabo de Peñas
Luanco
Candás
Mina de Arnao
Salinas
Avilés
Piedrasblancas
Gijón ★ p. 76
La Concha de Artedo
Cudillero
Puerto de Vega
Luarca
Navia
Castro de Coaña
Pravia
Salas
Museo y Circuito Fernando Alonso
30km 30 mins
Oviedo ★ p. 91
Tinéu
Grado
Langreo
Mieres del Camín
205km, 2 hrs 15 mins
Cangas del Narcea
La Pola
Moreda
ASTURIAS
San Emiliano
Villablino

20 km
12.43 mi

MARCO POLO HIGHLIGHTS

★ **GIJÓN**
Not the most beautiful city in the north – but surely the most fun ➤ p. 76

★ **RIBADESELLA**
This small fishing town with long sandy beaches is home to Queen Letizia's biggest fans ➤ p. 88

★ **CUEVA DE TITO BUSTILLO**
Not quite as famous as the Altamira cave – but you can actually go inside ➤ p. 88

★ **PLAYA DE GULPIYURI**
A beach that isn't by the sea? You'll find it here! ➤ p. 88

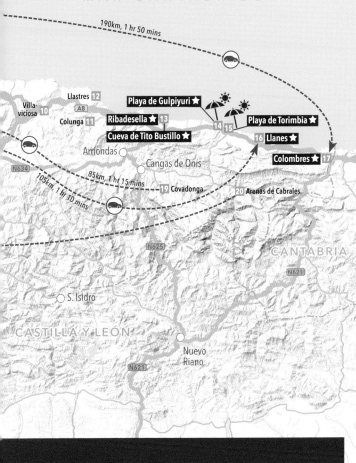

OCÉANO ATLÁNTICO

MAR CANTÁBRICO

190km, 1 hr 50 mins

Llastres 12

Villa-viciosa 10

A8

Colunga 11

Playa de Gulpiyuri ★

Ribadesella ★ 13

Playa de Torimbia ★

Cueva de Tito Bustillo ★

14 15

16 Llanes ★

Arriondas

Colombres ★ 17

N634

Cangas de Onís

85km, 1 hr 15 mins

19 Covadonga

20 Arenas de Cabrales

105km, 1 hr 10 mins

N625

CANTABRIA

N621

S. Isidro

CASTILLA Y LEÓN

Nuevo Riaño

N621

★ **PLAYA DE TORIMBIA**
Idyllic shell-shaped beach where clothing
is optional ➤ p. 88

★ **LLANES**
This pleasant holiday resort near the Picos
is a popular film location ➤ p. 89

★ **COLOMBRES**
This pretty, quiet locale is a real *"Indiano"*
village ➤ p. 90

★ **OVIEDO**
Asturias's medieval capital has a thriving
student scene ➤ p. 91

GIJÓN

Cimavilla

Museo Casa Natal de Jovellanos

Museo Termas Romanas de Campo Valdés

Ria de los Vagones

Museo Barjola

El Recetario

El Paralelo

Acuario de Gijón

El Feudo

C. Corrida

Calle Cabrales

Ciudadela de Celestino Solar

Museo del Ferrocarril de Asturias

Avenida Rufo García R

Av. de Juan Carlos I

Calle Sanz Crespo

Calle Ezcurdia

Café Dindurra

Calle Uría

Bi

Museo Nicanor Piñole

Avenida de Portugal

Magnus Blikstad

Avenida de la Constitución

de Schulz

Avenida de la Costa

Av. de Portugal

Calle Carlos Marx

Avenida Manuel Llaneza

Avenida

Calle San José

Calle Caveda

Avenida Pablo Iglesias

Calle Cienfuegos

Calle Alarcón

Calle Balme

500 m
547 yd

Calle Pérez de Ayala

Calle Ramón y Cajal

Calle Leopoldo Alas

Calle Feijóo

GIJÓN

(▢ J3) ★ **Gijón (272,000 inhabitants) is hardly a classical beauty – but it is decidedly eclectic. Just don't forget your windbreaker when you visit as it can get very gusty!**

The city has two large sandy beaches with a choice of views over the charming marina or the industrial docks. It also boasts an old fishing quarter full of lovely squares, as well as a chic city centre with car parks, café terraces, pubs, cultural hubs and crowds of hipsters in the streets.

WHERE TO START?

The **Plaza Mayor**! Unless you fall straight into one of the *sidrerías* in and around the main square, it's the best place to start if you want to explore the fishing neighbourhood of Cimavilla and most of the city's attractions. And Playa San Lorenzo is right round the corner. The train and bus stations are just a few hundred metres from the centre as well. If you want a central place to park your car, head to El Espigón Fomento, Jardines del Náutico or Playa de Poniente car parks.

Muséu del Pueblu d'Asturies

Laboral Ciudad de la Cultura

Calle Ezcurdia

Carretera de Villaviciosa

Jardín Botánico Atlántico

Carretera de La Providencia

Carretera Piles al Infanzón

Paseo Dr. Fleming

SIGHTSEEING

ACUARIO DE GIJÓN 👶

The aquarium with its artificial rocky landscapes is great fun for kids. (Make sure they don't reach into the tanks though: touching the sea anemones could cause burning and itching!) The aquarium features native fish from the Cantabrian Sea as well as the more exotic ones like clownfish (Nemo) and blue tang (Dory). The best bit is the escalator to the lower floor, where you can look up into a big tank of sharks. *Staggered opening times, see website | 17 euros, children 8.90 euros | Playa de Poniente | acuariogijon.es | ⏱ 1–1½ hrs*

CIMAVILLA

Looming majestically at the entrance to Cimavilla peninsula, with its historic fishing neighbourhood, to the left of the Plaza Mayor, is the *Palacio de Revillagigedo* from 1702, one of the city's main landmarks. In front of it is the equally majestic memorial to Don Pelayo, who founded the first Christian state after the Muslim conquest of the Iberian Peninsula, which spelled the beginning of the Christian *Reconquista*. But tourists are more often drawn to the nearby *Árbol de la Sidra*. This "tree" consists of 3,200 cider bottles, which is equivalent to the number of used bottles thrown away by 100 families in a year and is intended to encourage recycling. Just a few paces away is a leafy square on which the Casa Natal de Jovellanos is located (see below). Behind the Jovellanos museum, the streets become much shabbier and more run-down. The scent of weed lingers in the air and there are shops and pubs that the self-styled hipsters wouldn't set foot in. At the end is a park featuring at its highest point the sculpture *Elogio del Horizonte* by Eduardo Chillida. It stands on the remains of some fortifications that were begun in 1902 but never completed.

CIUDADELA DE CELESTINO SOLAR 🐖

Stuck in a 30m² hut with 11 other men? That's how it used to be in the *ciudadelas* of Gijón. With the explosion of industrialisation in the late 19th century, huge numbers of workers poured into the city, and they needed a roof over their heads. Business-minded (and unscrupulous) entrepreneurs then constructed these miniscule barrack-style bungalows with communal toilets for about 100 people each. Celestino Solar was one of them. His *ciudadela* was built in 1877, and entire families often lived in the tiny houses. This might sound like something out of a Dickens novel, but it remained the case until 1977!

The Ciudadela de Celestino Solar is the only example in Gijón where a few houses still remain. You can walk among the crumbling walls, look at the temporary exhibitions on the woeful conditions of Gijón's working class and see the meagre furnishings in old workers' housing. The cartoons at the entrance to the settlement make the whole thing seem rather cute, but the reality was very different. *April–Sept Tue–Sun 11am–7pm,*

Oct–March 11.30am–6.30pm | free admission | C/ Capua 13 | gijon.es | ⊙ *30 mins*

JARDÍN BOTÁNICO ATLÁNTICO
The botanical gardens are a dream – and not just for flower enthusiasts. Make sure you leave plenty of time for visiting these huge grounds: firstly, because there are so many interesting things to discover about the plant world, and secondly, because the route map is so complicated it'll take you hours to figure it out – if you manage it at all! the *Jardín de la Isla* is not to be missed: the oldest part of grounds dates to the 19th century, with its water lilies, bridges and pergolas. It's so romantic you'll want to sit down on a bench and dream of love. *Tue–Sun 10am–6pm, mid-May–mid-Sept*

INSIDER TIP
Romantic strolling

Jellyfish float serenely behind glass in Gijón's aquarium

until 9pm, July/Aug also Mon | 2.90 euros | Av. del Jardín Botánico 2230 | botanico.gijon.es | ⊙ 2–3 hrs

LABORAL CIUDAD DE LA CULTURA

Wow – what a huge building! Constructed during the Franco era, the megalomaniac University of Gijón was designed as a city within a city and is considered to be the largest building in Spain. In addition to the university, it houses research and cultural centres. Large parts of the gigantic complex are freely accessible to visitors. The Plaza Mayor is particularly impressive, with its 130m tower, round church and theatre. *See website for dates of guided tours | 6 euros | C/ Luis Moya Blanco 261 | laboralciudaddelacultura.com | ⊙ 1–1½ hrs*

MUSEO BARJOLA 🐷

Outside it's a palace from 1676. Inside it's an ultra-modern building featuring a collection of modern art and temporary exhibitions. The third floor is dedicated to Juan Barjola (1919–2004), whose work shows an ambivalent relationship with bullfighting. There is also an impressive chapel, which can be seen when you visit the temporary exhibition. *Tue–Sat 11.30am–1.30pm and 5–8pm, Sun noon–2pm | free admission | C/ Trinidad 17 | museobarjola. es | ⊙ 1 hrs*

INSIDER TIP Exciting exhibitions in the chapel

MUSEO CASA NATAL DE JOVELLANOS 🐷

The Asturians worship Gaspar Melchor de Jovellanos (1744–1811) with a cult-like fervour – mainly because he fought tirelessly for the social welfare of the population. And the fact he survived several assassination attempts probably boosted his hero status even more. But if you think visiting his birthplace will teach you more about this statesman, poet and writer, you would be mistaken. The house does feature the bedstead of this intellectual of the Spanish Enlightenment, but otherwise the museum is a motley collection of different art styles and eras: alongside a little modernism, a lot of Spanish romance and some slightly kitsch realism, you will also find some Old Masters and a few very weird sculptures, like *Fórmula 1* by José María Navascués (1934–1979). It is meant to be a tribute to motor racing but looks more like a perverted sex toy. One really impressive sculpture is the wood-carved *Retablo del Mar* by Sebastián Miranda (1885-1975). It shows a harbour scene in the fishing quarter of Cimavilla and is a treasure trove of hidden objects. The museum building itself, a traditional 16th-century Asturian palace, is worth seeing too. *Tue–Fri 9.30am–2pm and 5-7.30pm, Sat/Sun 10am–2pm and 5-7.30pm | free admission | Plaza de Jovellanos | gijon.es | ⊙ 1–1½ hrs*

MUSEO DEL FERROCARRIL DE ASTURIAS 🐷

A trainspotter's paradise: the former railway station is home to a range of locomotives and carriages from the early years of Asturian rail travel to the present day. *Tue–Fri 9.30am–2pm and 5–7.30pm, Sat/Sun 10am–2pm and 5–7.30pm | free admission | Plaza Estación del Norte | gijon.es | ⊙ 1 hr*

MUSÉU DEL PUEBLU D'ASTURIES

"Everything you ever wanted to know about Asturias…" This museum about the Asturian people features around 20 mansions and farmhouses, barns and stores, shepherd huts and a *sidra* press, which you can visit and go inside. It also has exhibitions on history and culture, religious customs, and a very extensive one on the *gaita*, the Asturian bagpipes, in the ⚑ *Museo de la Gaita* connected to the open-air museum. The main building is the impressive Asturias Pavilion from Expo 1992 in Seville, where you can travel back in time to learn about Asturian cuisine and eating habits from 1800 to 1965. The museum also features the first showers used in Asturias, which are equally (if not more) fascinating. *April–Sept Tue–Fri 10am–7pm, Sat/Sun 10.30am–7pm; Oct–March Tue–Fri 9.30am–6.30pm, Sat/Sun 10am–6.30pm | free admission | Paseo del Doctor Fleming 877 | redmeda.com | ⊙ 2–3 hrs*

MUSEO NICANOR PIÑOLE

Even if you've never heard of him, this museum is still worth a visit! Housed in the building of a former preschool from 1904, it displays a large selection of works from the Gijón-born painter. And it is very varied because Piñole (1878–1978) lived to be 100 years old. This means that the pictures, quite apart from their artistic merit, are historical documents showing Asturian history, including rural and working-class life as well as the horrors of the Civil War. *Tue–Fri 9.30am–2pm and 5–7.30pm, Sat/Sun 10am–2pm and 5–7.30pm | free admission | Plaza de Europa 28 | gijon.es | ⊙ 1 hr*

MUSEO TERMAS ROMANAS DE CAMPO VALDÉS

This museum features Roman thermal baths dating back to the first or second century. When going round the various excavations, you can press buttons to illuminate different areas. But watch out: some parts of the ceiling are so low that anyone who isn't a child is at risk of banging their head. *Tue–Fri 9.30am–2pm and 5–7.30pm, Sat/Sun 10am–2pm and 5–7.30pm | free admission | Campo Valdés | gijon. es | ⊙ 30 mins*

EATING & DRINKING

BISTRO 21

If you've got wanderlust, this is the perfect place for you: tasty dishes from distant lands will send you on a flavour journey. It's all prepared with Asturian ingredients and lots of love for nature. *Tue/Wed closed | C/ Aguado 21 | tel. 9 84 19 18 75 | bistro21.es | €–€€*

CAFÉ DINDURRA

This café with terrace at the Teatro Jovellanos is the oldest in Gijón,

The shopping street Calle San Bernardo starts from this arcade on the Plaza Mayor

dating back to 1901, and is a bit of a cult favourite. Live music at the weekend. *Daily | Paseo de Begoña 11 | dindurra.es*

EL FEUDO

Pretty, very busy and popular restaurant serving Asturian cuisine with modern presentation and affordable prices. Make sure you book in advance! *Mon closed | C/ Felipe Menéndez 4 | tel. 9 85 35 16 59 | elfeudogijon.com | €–€€*

EL PARALELO

Sleek wine bar with a small, select menu. The *patatas rellenas* (potatoes stuffed with mince) are particularly delicious. *Sun closed | C/ La Merced/C/ Anghera | tel. 9 84 51 44 36 | FB | €*

EL RECETARIO

Right by the Plaza Mayor, this place offers jazzed-up takes on Spanish classics with specially selected ingredients. *Tue/Wed closed | C/ Trinidad 1 | tel. 9 84 08 28 94 | elrecetariodealex. com | €–€€*

SHOPPING

The *Calles Los Moros, Corrida* and *San Bernardo* are home to Zara & Co. and, thankfully, plenty of independent shops as well. At *San Bernardo 91* you will find the delicatessen *Puerta del Sol* selling the finest Asturian specialities. It has been run by three generations of the Vega family. If your

INSIDER TIP
Delicious Asturias

feet are sore, head to the *Paseo Begoña* and collapse on one of their chairs (or just carry on shopping there).

BEACHES

Gijón has two city beaches, the 1.5km *Playa de Poniente* with a not-very-majestic view over the industrial docks and the equally long *Playa de San Lorenzo* and its promenade that's great for ambling along when the beach vanishes at high tide.

NIGHTLIFE

Watching football is a must in Spain, and you can do so at *La Bull 2 bar (C/ San Bernardo 15)*. If you prefer to sit at the marina in style and sip cocktails, go to the chic bar *Ócean (Plaza Puerto Deportivo | ocean-gijon.com)*. One of the trendiest and, at the same time, most traditional places where you can go for drinks until well after midnight is the *Varsovia (C/ Cabrales 18 | varsoviagijon.com)* in a magnificent modernist building with a vintage atmosphere.

AROUND GIJÓN

1 CABO DE PEÑAS
30km northwest of Gijón/35 mins via the AS 19 and AS 118
This place feels like the end of the world. Make sure you wear a warm jumper – there's always a bitter wind

here. But the view of the coast from the foot of the lighthouse is unparalleled. On the ground floor there is a small information centre where you can experience a simulated storm at sea with the help of a makeshift fan and lots of noise from the crackling loudspeakers. Multimedia, back-of-beyond style. You can also find out everything there is to know about this stretch of coast and its inhabitants. *April–Sept daily 10.30am–1.30pm and 4.30–7pm, Oct–March 10am–2pm and 4.30–6pm | 1 euro | unviaje creativo.com |* ⊙ *30 mins |* ⊞ *J3*

2 AVILÉS
30km west of Gijón/25 mins via the A 8
Here in the city of Avilés (83,000 inhabitants), it could be said that they live according to the motto: "What the Basques can do, we can do too!" And so this declining industrial town also has its own arts and culture centre. But, while the Guggenheim Museum sparked an upturn in Bilbao's tourism, the same can't be said for Avilés (yet). The audacious *Centro Niemeyer (centroniemeyer.org)* on the edge of the harbour was designed by Brazilian architect Oscar Niemeyer and looks just like half a boiled egg. The spacious, tarmacked grounds are popular with young people for skating and cycling. But the lack of exciting exhibitions and resulting lack of crowds mean the risk of accidents is rather low…

It's usually enough to admire Niemeyer's "egg" from the outside if you're taking a walk through the old town. For an old industrial town, it's surprisingly beautiful: green spaces, a covered market by the docks in the middle of a square framed by glass façades, an imposing Plaza Mayor and countless listed houses with arcades. Unfortunately, a lot of shops stand vacant and many of the residents are conspicuously poor. Hopefully the cultural centre will be a golden egg after all! ▥ H3

3 SALINAS & MINA DE ARNAO
35km west of Gijón/30 mins via the A 8 and N 632
The spa town of *Salinas* (4,500 inhabitants) with its 3km of beach has been treasured by Asturians since the 19th century and is now a surfers' paradise. On the way there from Avilés, you will start by driving for what feels like an eternity through dockyards and industrial plants. When you're convinced

you've taken a wrong turning, you suddenly hit the scenic landscapes again. To your right, you will see a stretch of dunes with a wooden walkway through the nature reserve along the seashore. Cyclists can take the beautiful bike path.

Salinas itself is sedate and dignified (if you ignore a few ugly skyscrapers) and exudes calculated boredom. At the western edge of the town is a peninsula with the open-air 🐦 *Museo de las Anclas Philippe Cousteau (free access and admission)*, a colourful, rather crude mix of anchors and whimsical artistic declarations of love for the sea.

Immediately behind the anchor museum there is a single-track former railway tunnel (only drive through on green!) into another world. Above the Playa de Arnao is the 🏊 *Mina de Arnao (June–Sept Tue–Sun 11am–3pm and*

Centro Niemeyer in Avilés

4–8pm; Oct–May 11am–2pm and 4–6.30pm | 4.50 euros | C/ La Mina 7 | tel. 9 85 50 77 99 | museominade arnao.es | ⏲ 1½–2 hrs), where the dilapidated industrial buildings and abandoned villas are being slowly reclaimed by nature, creating a ghostly, eerie atmosphere. Opened in 1833, the mine was closed in 1915 because seawater began to seep in. It is the oldest coal mine in the Iberian Peninsula and the only submarine mine in Europe. Today you can take a guided tour of the almost 200-year-old mine and delve deep into the industrial history of Asturias. Make sure to book in advance because access is limited. ⎙ H3

4 CUDILLERO

55km west of Gijón/45 mins via the A 8

If you like a bit of hustle and bustle, this place is for you. This picturesque fishing village with colourful cottages nestled on steep hillsides is one of the few places in Asturias where tourists flock even outside the high season. If you manage to snag a table somewhere, be sure to try the seafood: Cudillero is famous for its fish restaurants. At *Sidrería El Remo (closed Mon evening and Tue | C/ Fuente de Abajo 9 | tel. 9 85 59 02 18 | sidreriaelremo. com | €€)*, for example, you can enjoy a view of the harbour, cider and delicious *paella de marisco* all at the same time. Or, if you're brave enough, try the local speciality ⚑ *curadillo*, or dried shark. ⎙ H3

INSIDER TIP
Cut your teeth on some shark!

5 LA CONCHA DE ARTEDO 🏖

55km west of Gijón/45 mins via the A 8

Every region has its shell-shaped beach. The 700m *Concha* beach in Asturias might not be half as chic as the one in San Sebastián, but it's still beautiful. Don't be put off by the concrete pillars of the viaduct at the exit! Along the Río Uncín, there is a 1.3km circular walking route, part of which consists of a wooden walkway to the beach and back. The wetland nature reserve is home to happy ducks, and the terrace of the restaurant and bar *Casa Miguel (daily in the summer | tel. 9 85 59 63 50 | casamiguella conchadeartedo.es | €–€€)* has something of a Caribbean feel to it with the breeze rustling the nearby eucalyptus trees and the waves lapping against the shore. On the downside, the beach is stony. ⎙ H3

6 LUARCA

90km west of Gijón/1 hr via the A 8

Luarca (4,800 inhabitants) was once swarming with pirates. Was? Even today this town surrounded by looming rocks gives the impression that you might spot a pirate or two. And it's not just the buccaneering ways of some restaurant proprietors who claim that everything on the menu is off – apart from the extortionately priced fish of the day. The cemetery is situated high up, accessed by a winding road which is so steep you'll be worried about joining the deceased a little sooner than you bargained for. And you wouldn't be in bad company: the cemetery is home to Luarca-born

Book in advance if you want to secure an outside table at one of Cudillero's restaurants

Nobel Prize winner Severo Ochoa (1905–1993), who has several memorials and plaques dedicated to him in the town. Aside from this, Luarca also has a tang of fish and fishing in the air and the terraces of harbourside bars are frequented by hardened seamen relaxing after a day's work. The romantics among you will want to visit the Bridge of the Kiss. According to legend, the pirate Cambaral was captured and injured, and the daughter of the Lord of Luarca nursed him back to health. Naturally, the two fell in love and decided to flee. When the old man gave chase and caught the love-birds at the harbour, they saw their last hour coming, embraced each other and sank into such a heartfelt kiss that the furious father cut off both

INSIDER TIP
Pirate romance meets a tragic end

their heads with a single blow. Today, the *Puente del Beso* crosses the water at the spot where the tragedy happened. Sigh... *G3*

7 PUERTO DE VEGA
100km west of Gijón/1 hr 5 mins via the A 8

If you're searching for that authentic fishing port atmosphere, look no further than Puerto de Vega (2,000 inhabitants), where the catch goes directly from the trawler to your plate. This means the place is usually a hive of activity, especially at the weekend, because Asturians from the surrounding area come here in droves to enjoy a meal. Restaurants like *La Marina (closed Mon | Paseo del Muelle | tel. 9 85 64 80 38 | lamarinapuerto devega.com | €€)* have been serving exquisite fish dishes since 1925, and at the lovely portside bar *El Chicote*

The best view of the Celtic settlement of Castro de Coaña is from the road

(closed Mon | C/ El Muelle 23 | tel. 9 85 64 80 35 | FB | €–€€) you can even find seafood at affordable prices.

The place is also home to a rather endearing museum, the 🐷 *Museo Etnográfico Juan Pérez Villamil (Tue–Fri noon–2pm and 5.30–7.30pm, Sat/Sun 11.30am–2.30pm and 4.30–7.30pm | free admission | Av. Juan Pérez Villamil 2 | redmeda.com | ⏱ 30–45 mins)*, a motley cabinet of curiosities housed in an old fish-canning factory, which contains collections including shells, film cameras, model ships, old furniture and traditional tools. A hologram explains about work in the fish factory, and an exhibition in a replica ship's hull provides information about the history of fishing and the art of canning. *▥ G3*

🟦 NAVIA

100km west of Gijón/1 hr 10 mins via the A 8

This lively port (8,500 inhabitants) with its small historic centre and several "Indian" villas is situated on the Ría de Navia, which flows into the sea surrounded by pine and eucalyptus trees. Along the Ría is a wooden walkway *(Paseo Marítimo)* to the *Playa de Navia*, which passes the lagoon *La Poza*, a favoured rest stop for water birds. *▥ G3*

🟦 CASTRO DE COAÑA

105km northwest of Gijón/1¼ hrs via the A 8

Honestly, these remains of a first-century Celtic hilltop settlement, complete with about 100 round or oval-shaped cottages, are probably easier to see from the road leading up to them than from inside the settlement itself. But go inside anyway and support Asturian tourism. They have a hard enough time of it as it is. *Wed–Sun 10.30am–3.30pm, April–Sept until 5.30pm | 3.13 euros | ⏱ 1 hr | ⅏ G3*

⑩ VILLAVICIOSA
30km east of Gijón/25 mins via the A 8
This town (14,500 inhabitants) is known for its many cider manufacturers. So make a pitstop and order yourself a glass, which will be poured from a height! But be sure to stop at one, not more, because the road to the next stop at Colunga, while beautiful, is perilously steep, narrow and winding – that is if you take the worthwhile detour via the AS 332, which stretches far inland and eventually becomes the A 258. ⅏ *J3*

⑪ COLUNGA
45km east of Gijón/35 mins via the A 8
Apart from a few "Indian" palaces and its dinosaur museum, the town of Colunga (3,500 inhabitants) is nice but nothing to write home about. A little way out of town in *Gobiendes* is a tiny nature reserve centre called *Centro de Interpretación de la Sierra del Sueve (staggered opening times, see website | 1 euro | sierradelsueve. es | ⏱ 30 mins)*. The reserve probably only gets about ten visitors a year, but if you go out the door and up the stairs, there is a viewing platform with a stunning view of the mountains – the Sierra del Sueve itself.

INSIDER TIP
Mountain view just for you

From the outside, the ☎ *Museo del Jurásico de Asturias MUJA (staggered opening times, see website | 7.21 euros, children aged 4-11 4.75 euros | Rasa de San Telmo | museo jurasicoasturias.com | ⏱ 1½–2 hrs)* looks like a clutch of alien eggs – which is rather fitting. There are also life-size models of dinosaurs all around. They're not for touching and definitely not for climbing, but the Spanish kids don't care a jot for the rules. You're also supposed to keep quiet inside, which the little terrors take as the perfect opportunity to shriek to their hearts' content. In summary: the dinosaur museum is kid-heaven.

There's plenty of educational stuff too, of course. The part about the dinosaur finds in Asturias on the Costa de los Dinosaurios, to which the museum owes its existence, is particularly interesting. There are fossils, replicas, huge bone structures, and a rather eye-catching main attraction: a pair of life-size T-Rexes going at it like rabbits. Parents be warned: you'll might some explaining to do. ⅏ *K3*

⑫ LLASTRES
45km east of Gijón/40 mins via the A 8 and AS 257
The problem with this quaint fishing village (2,000 inhabitants, also spelled Lastres) is that when you've scrambled down all the steep alleys and steps to get to the centre of this historic, heritage-protected place, you'll have to climb them all back up again afterwards – or vice versa. But the sweaty ascent is well worth it, though you'll

sometimes feel as if you're on a Greek island rather than in Spain. Right at the top is the viewpoint *Mirador de San Roque* at the eponymous 17th-century chapel, giving you stunning views of the harbour, beach, ocean and the whole surrounding area. If you're interested in curiosities, check out the arms and legs made of plastic and wax hanging on the wall of the chapel next to San Roque. They look as if they could be used for some voodoo ritual – faith (or superstition) can have some strange manifestations. *K3*

13 RIBADESELLA ★

65km east of Gijón/55 mins via the A 8

This fishing town (5,700 inhabitants) with a large beach is looked over by two hermitages. You can climb up to them if you like, but it's more relaxing to sit in one of the pretty squares of the historic old town and devour a couple of ⚐ *letizias*. Because some of the famous queen's family members are from this area and she enjoyed spending her holidays here, the local confectioners invented the *letizia* to mark the beginning of her reign. This sweet treat can take the form of a buttery pastry in the shape of a heart or a giant sweet mess made with marzipan, custard filling and orange cream. The important thing is that it bears the royal name.

Ribadesella is also known for its *sidrerías* and *marisquerías* serving seaside specialities. A dependable option is *La Parrilla (closed Mon | C/ de Palacio Valdés 33 | tel. 9 85 86 02 88 | laparrilladeribadesella.com | €€–€€€).*

It has a cosy, welcoming atmosphere and you can enjoy fish and seafood, such as the delicious, highly sought-after and rare (read: expensive) *percebes*, or barnacles.

To the southwest of the town is one of the main attractions in all of Asturias: the ★ *Cueva de Tito Bustillo (staggered opening times, see website | 5.45 euros | Av. de Tito Bustillo | centrotitobustillo.com | ⏱ 1–2 hrs)* with its 20,000-year-old rock paintings, which is a UNESCO World Heritage Site. To protect the paintings, access to the cave is strictly limited. It's best to book online days or even weeks in advance of your visit. And if you don't manage to get tickets to the cave itself, you can learn all there is to know about it at the information centre. *K3*

14 PLAYA DE GULPIYURI ★ 🌴

75km east of Gijón/55 mins via the A 8

This 40m-long beach is the shortest in Asturias. But in fact, it isn't really a beach at all; instead, it is a sinkhole in the karst rock. The sinkhole is around 100m back from the coastline, but at high tide it floods with sea water through underground caves in the surrounding rocks, so it is still tidal here. It's a natural landmark and provides a unique swimming experience that is only accessible on foot. *K3*

15 PLAYA DE TORIMBIA ★ 🌴

80km to Niembro east of Gijón/1 hr 5 mins via the A 8

The 500m Playa de Torimbia with its almost-perfect shell-shaped arc is one of the most beautiful beaches in

Northern Spain. It can be reached on foot from the nearby village of *Niembro* (which is also worth a detour for its picturesque church and waterfront cemetery). Right next to this naturist beach (clothes are permitted too), by a coastal cliff, is another very beautiful beach that can also only be accessed on foot: the 300m *Playa de Toranda*. ▢ *L3*

🔢 LLANES ⭐

90km east of Gijón/1 hr 5 mins via the A 8

Summer visitors are particularly fond of this fishing town (13,500 inhabitants) in the foothills of the Sierra de Cuera. After all, there are 30 great beaches nearby and the Picos de Europa aren't far away either. The small medieval old town with its churches, palaces, towers and the ruins of its city walls feels like a land that time forgot. No wonder several films have been shot here.

INSIDER TIP
Go for a paddle, like Hugh Grant

The *Itinerarios de Cine* tour takes you to 25 film locations in and around Llanes. For example, the tour goes via the *Playa de Borizu* where Hugh Grant set foot in 1987, and the *Indiana* villa Palacio de Partarríu, which Juan Antonio Bayona used to film the cult horror flick *The Orphanage (El Orfanato, 2007)*. You can find a route map at the tourist information centre.

The *Cubos de la Memoria* by artist Agustín Ibarrola, who enjoyed painting the waves in the harbour in rainbow colours, are rather a matter of taste. For some, they are a landmark of the town and an outstanding work of art depicting the history and culture of the place; for others, they're a bunch of annoying paint splotches.

A large beach, a pretty old town and plenty of cider: Ribadesella

The Archivo de Indianos in Colombres is a prime example of Asturian "Indian" architecture

Of course, this lovely fishing town also has lovely fish, and you can find particularly good ones at *El Bálamu* (daily in summer | tel. 9 85 41 36 06 | FB | €€) by the fishing harbour. *Retiro* (closed Tue and all evenings except Fri/Sat | Carretera Pancar | tel. 9 85 40 02 40 | elretirollanes.es | €€–€€€) in nearby *Pancar* even has a Michelin star. *▥ L3*

▯ COLOMBRES ★ ▰

110km east of Gijón/1¼ hrs via the A 8

This village, seemingly frozen in time like Sleeping Beauty, is a really treasure trove of "Indian" architecture that has been unusually well preserved. The *La Huella Indiana* tour (route map at the tourist information centre and in the Casa de Cultura, which is also an old *Indiana* palace) takes you to the most impressive buildings and tells the story of the people who constructed them.

The *Archivo de Indianos – Museo de la Emigración* (Tue–Sun 10am–2pm and 4–7pm, July/Aug until 8pm | 8 euros | Quinta Guadalupe | archivodeindianos.es | ⊙ 1 hrs) is housed in a palace from 1906 – a prime example of "Indian" architecture – surrounded by a park in which some of the plants were imported from America. Nosy visitors can peep into old suitcases and see what possessions the emigrants would have taken with them. On the second floor, there are some distressing pictures of the emigrants who drowned in shipwrecks during the crossing, including of the big steamer *Príncipe de Asturias*, which sank in 1916 killing 445 people. *▥ L3*

INSIDER TIP
Discover the "Spanish Titanic"

OVIEDO

(山 H-J3) ★ **Oviedo (221,000 inhabitants), the capital of the Kingdom of Asturias, has a picture-perfect historic centre with myriad little squares and is considered the cleanest city in Spain.**

You can see all the sights in one day because everything is within walking distance. But it would be a shame to rush. Instead, take your time and have a seat on one of the pub terraces in the Plaza Alfonso II or the Plaza Mayor and watch the world go by against the backdrop of the picturesque city. The university, which dates back to the 16th century, has brought with it countless bars, book shops and young people in the streets.

SIGHTSEEING

CAMPO DE SAN FRANCISCO

The large city park, which was once the garden of a monastery, is a green oasis at the heart of Oviedo. The per-golas, sculptures, little ponds and ancient trees would create the perfect moment of calm – if it weren't for the free-roaming peacocks squawking at the top of their lungs. The ruins of the portal of the Romanesque church of San Isidoro in amongst the gardens create the perfect romantic mood. A tip for small visitors: you will find the comic-book character Mafalda sitting on a bench beside a duckpond. She is look-ing forward to meeting you.

INSIDER TIP
Feed the ducks with Mafalda

MERCADO & PLAZA EL FONTÁN 🐦

This pleasant corner of the old town becomes a thriving hub of hustle and bustle on market day. Near the late 19th-century covered market, there is a square containing the rather attractive sculpture *La Bella Lola*. The streets around the plaza are full of traders hawking their wares. The many flower stands around the edge of the Plaza Fontán are particularly lovely to look at.

MUSEO ARQUEOLÓGICO DE ASTURIAS 🐖

The origins of this former monastery, which houses the city's archaeological museum, date back to the eighth cen-tury. The cloister harks back to this time and features deceased members of the nobility carved in stone. In addi-tion, the place exhibits what seems like everything that has ever been found in Asturias, with pieces from the Neanderthals and the Iron Age to the Roman era and the Middle Ages. The life-size replica of a female

INSIDER TIP
Sloshed in the Stone Age?!

WHERE TO START?

The best place is **Plaza Alfonso II** with its single-tower cathedral, because this will allow you to soak up the medieval feel of the city and from here you can walk to almost all the sights (and pubs and shops) in just a few minutes. The same goes for the train station, and the bus station is only a few hundred metres further away.

Neanderthal from the Valle de Sidral looks as if she might have drunk too much *sidra*. *Wed–Fri 9.30am–8pm, Sat 9.30am–2pm and 5–8pm, Sun 9.30am–3pm | free admission | C/ San Vicente 3–5 | museoarqueologicodeasturias.com |* ⏱ *1½ hrs*

MUSEO DE BELLAS ARTES DE ASTURIAS 🐦

Caution: you'll probably get lost here! The museum is made up of several medieval palaces with modern extensions connected by a maze of staircases and corridors. It houses a Picasso, a Miró, a Dalí, Goya engravings and some kitschy old art from the region, as well as some really exciting modern works. The paintings by "master of light" Joaquín Sorolla are particularly eye-catching. *Sept–June Tue–Fri 10.30am–2pm and 4.30–8.30pm, Sat 11.30am–2pm and 5–8pm, Sun 11.30am–2.30pm; July/ Aug Tue–Sat 10.30am–2pm and 4–8pm, Sun 10.30am–2.30pm | free admission | Palacio de Velarde, C/ de Santa Ana 1 | museobbaa.com |* ⏱ *2–3 hrs*

SAN SALVADOR DE OVIEDO CATHEDRAL

This late-Gothic cathedral from the 14th century has several gold altars, a beautiful cloister with a creepy, dark crypt and the *Cámara Santa*, which contains valuable church treasures. This "holy chamber" has been barricaded shut with a thick iron cross since the late 1970s, when it was targeted by some particularly brazen thieves. The rooms with the depictions of saints – contorted with pain and suffering as is typical for Spain – are the stuff of nightmares. Incidentally, the cathedral has only one tower because there was no money left after the first one was completed in the 16th century. *Opening times change often, see website | 7 euros | Plaza Alfonso II El Casto | catedraldeoviedo.com |* ⏱ *1 hr*

EATING & DRINKING

BODEGA EL MOLINÓN

Tapas bar lauded for its speciality sausages. Large selection, low prices and occasional live music. *Sun evening and Wed closed | C/ Águila 13 | tel. 9 84 06 15 89 | €*

CASA FERMÍN

Beautiful, elegant restaurant with equally beautiful and elegant Spanish cuisine with innovative flair. *Sun/ Mon closed | C/ San Francisco 8 | tel. 9 85 21 64 52 | casafermin.com | €€–€€€*

EL RAITÁN

Traditional, cosy establishment with down-to-earth Asturian fare. Their speciality is onions stuffed with tuna. Make sure you stay for a digestif afterwards! *Sun evening and Tue/Wed closed | Plaza Trascorrales 5 | tel. 9 84 08 59 72 | elraitanoviedo.com | €–€€*

PER SE CAFÉ & CO.

A super cosy, vintage, studenty café in a historic building. You can sit out on the terrace or in the inner courtyard, or lounge on the sofas inside and enjoy a piece of Guinness tart or maybe a

OVIEDO

Calle Jovellanos

🍴 Bodega El Molinón

Museo Arqueológico de Asturias 📍

Calle Schultz

Cathedral 📍
San Salvador de Oviedo

Museo de 📍
Bellas Artes de Asturias

📍 Campo
San Francisco

🍴 Casa Fermín
C. San Francisco

Per Se 🍴
Café & Co.

🍴 El Raitán

📍 Mercado &
Plaza El Fontán

100 m
109 yd

Jägermeister brownie. *Daily | C/ Canoniga 18 | FB*

SIDRERÍAS

The huge cider barrel at the entrance to the *Calle Gascona* is a clear indication that the "Bulevar de la Sidra" is entirely dedicated to cider. One of the best and most popular *sidrerías* here is *Tierra Astur (C/ Gascona 1 | tierra-astur.com)*.

SHOPPING

Most of the shopping happens around the central *Calle Uría*. Here, you will find the shopping centre *El Corte Inglés (C/ Uría 9)* – there's another one in the *Centro Comercial Salesas (C/ Nueve de Mayo 2)* – along with the other usual suspects. Since 1930,

Oviedo has been famous for its legendary bonbons and other sweets from *Peñalba (C/ Milicias Nacionales 4)*, which make the perfect souvenir. Regional culinary specialities can be found at the ☂ *Mercado El Fontán (mercadofontan. es)*. The area is also crammed with book shops.

NIGHTLIFE

The *Teatro Campoamor* opera house *(C/ Pelayo 3 | teatrocampoamor.es)*, built in 1892, is steeped in history and offers a colourful programme of concerts, operas and theatre. The *Calle Mon* and *Calle Oscura* behind the cathedral are a hub of student parties at night. In most clubs, the party doesn't start until 11.30pm and goes

How to pour Asturian *sidra*

champion Fernando Alonso. Exhibits range from the kart this Oviedo-born star used to drive laps in as a young boy, to the wheels he raced with in the premier class. *Daily 10am–7pm | 15 euros, children (12 and under) 10 euros | museoycircuitofernando alonso.com | ⏱ 1–2 hrs | ▥ J3*

on until the early hours, often accompanied by live music. If you fancy a boogie, head to the bar and club *Kapital (C/ Cimadevilla 15)* or *Salsipuedes (C/ Ildefonso Martínez 7)*.

AROUND OVIEDO

🔞 MUSEO Y CIRCUITO FERNANDO ALONSO 👹
10km north of Oviedo/15 mins via the AS II
The place to be if you have a need for speed. This museum in *Cayés* has a wide range of items relating to the first Spanish Formula 1 world

🔞 COVADONGA
85km east of Oviedo/1½ hrs via Cangas de Onís
The five million full parking spaces, hostels, bars and pubs along the route into the mountains are the first clue that this mythical pilgrimage site is often sheer pandemonium. The main attraction is the *Santa Cueva*, the Holy Grotto with the sarcophagus of the nobleman Pelayo, who vanquished the Moors in the Battle of Covadonga in CE 718 or 722 (no one is sure which). This battle is considered the start of the *Reconquista*, the Christian reconquest of Spain, which had its roots here in the Asturian mountains in the eighth century. The tomb isn't obvious at first glance; it is situated, rather irreverently, in a roughly hewn hole in the rock. Nearby is the impressive neo-Romanesque *Basílica de Covadonga*.

Directly behind Covadonga is a barrier that is supposed to prevent access (when the weather is poor) to the Lagos de Covadonga, which lie at the heart of the Picos de Europa at a height of around 1,000m. But no one really checks. It's true that driving to the two mountain lakes *Lago de Enol* and *Lago de la Ercina* can be fatal. The sides of the extremely narrow roads that run along a sheer drop are barely secured, if at all. What is more, the fog can descend in a matter of seconds, and when it is particularly thick you can't see your hand in front of your face – let alone the free-roaming cows, donkeys, goats and chickens that make themselves at home in the middle of the road. It's much better to hike up on foot when the weather is good. There are several signposted paths. If you make it to the top, it's well worth it: the views of the two lakes and out over the Picos are incredible. *K4*

20 ARENAS DE CABRALES
105km east of Oviedo/1¾ hrs via Cangas de Onís
This town (2,000 inhabitants) is a popular starting point for hikes in the Picos de Europa and is famous for Cabrales, a piquant blue sheep's cheese with a strong odour (it's best not to pack it in your suitcase!). If you want to learn more about the cheese and its history, you can take a guided tour of one of the natural caves where this delicious stinker matures. *Daily 10.15am–1.15pm and 4.15–6.15pm, April–Oct until 7.15pm, book by calling tel. 9 85 84 67 02 | 5 euros | Puente Cares | fundacion cabrales.com | 1 hr L4*

SLEEP WELL IN ASTURIAS

A NIGHT AT THE "INDIAN" PALACE
The *Palacio Arias (16 rooms | Av. des los Emigrantes 11 | tel. 9 85 47 36 71 | palacioarias.es | €)* was built in Navia in 1929; the owner at the time had made a fortune in Puerto Rico and had had this modest dwelling built upon his return. The lounges on the ground floor still have the original furnishings. Here, you can experience how *Indianos* would have lived or simply enjoy the beautiful gardens. Important: make sure you book a room in the palace itself – they have other rooms!

CHIC SLEEPING IN STYLE
Boutique hotel *El Môderne (47 rooms | C/ Marqués de San Esteban 27 | tel. 9 84 08 08 09 | elmoderne hotel.com | €€)* in the centre of Gijón has a real touch of class, from the elegant, minimalist furnishings in the spacious rooms and the stylish modern bathrooms to the chic yet delicious breakfasts.

GALICIA

FJORDS, WILD HORSES & PILGRIMS

The Spanish crooner Julio Iglesias is famous for singing "Un canto a Galicia" – which became an international hit – in *Galego*, a soft and melancholy regional language that sounds like a cross between Portuguese and Italian. It's achingly beautiful – just like pretty much everything in Galicia.

Rugged, romantic rock formations, precipitous cliffs, beaches that stretch for miles and, beyond it all, a lush green landscape strewn with patches of pale blue when the hydrangeas are in bloom. The

At high tide the Praia das Catedrais disappears under the waves

scenery is characterised by fjord-like bays called *rías*. And then, of course, punctuating this natural beauty are the towns and cities.

A Coruña, the *Ciudad de Cristal*, is a sophisticated seaside city. The rather gruff, industrial town of Vigo makes up for its lack of elegance with bags of character. And then, last but not least, there is the Galician capital, Santiago de Compostela, which hardly needs an introduction. And did you know that the most famous Galician of all was called Columbus?

GALICIA

OCÉANO ATLÁNTICO

MARCO POLO HIGHLIGHTS

★ **A CORUÑA**
The "glass city" exudes elegance and
sophistication ➤ p. 100

★ **TORRE DE HÉRCULES**
Climb the oldest lighthouse in the
world in A Coruña ➤ p. 103

★ **PRAIA DAS CATEDRAIS**
This beach is like a temple – but you
need a ticket during high season
➤ p. 108

★ **SANTIAGO DE COMPOSTELA**
A paradise for pilgrims – and others too
➤ p. 108

★ **ISLAS CÍES**
This national park has the most
beautiful beaches in Spain ➤ p. 114

★ **BAIONA**
Columbus's *La Pinta* docked here in
1493 – and it's still here today ➤ p. 114

★ **O GROVE**
One peninsula, 70 beaches. What more
could you ask for? ➤ p. 116

★ **CAMBADOS**
You don't need "wine goggles" to enjoy
this beautiful town ➤ p. 118

20 km
12.43 mi

MAR CANTÁBRICO

4 Cabo Ortegal
Cariño

Santo André
de Teixido **3**
Cedeira

Ortigueira

San Cibrao
Viveiro **5**   Sargadelos **6**   Burela

Praia das Catedrais ★ **7**
Ribadeo

Ferrol **2**   Narón
Fene

Mugardos

As Pontes de
García Rodríguez

Mondoñedo

Torre de Hércules ★

A Coruña ★
p. 100

1 Betanzos

Cullerredo

AG64

Vilalba

A8

Meira

A6

Guitiriz

Teixeiro

A8

Rábade

A Fonsagrada

N634

Ordes

GALICIA

Lugo

N640

Sobrado

Sigüeiro

AP9

Arzúa

Melide

A54

Becerreá

N547

Palas
de Rei

Portomarín

A6

155km, 1 hr 40 mins

Monterroso

Sarria

N640

Silleda

Taboada

Rodeiro

Lalín

Chantada

AG53

160km, 1 hr 40 mins

N525

Monforte
de Lemos

N540

Quiroga

O Carballiño

N120

Sober

320km, 3 hrs 15 mins

A Rúa

Ourense

A Pobra
de Trives

Covelo

Ribadavia

A52

A Cañiza

N525

Allariz

Viana do Bolo

Celanova

A52

Melgaço

A Gudiña

As Neves

Xinzo
de Limia

PORTUGAL

Bande

ESPAÑA

N525

Verín

A CORUÑA

(🗺 C3) **The radiant coastal city of ★ A Coruña (245,000 inhabitants) is known as the *Ciudad de Cristal* (City of Glass), because of its many balconies enclosed in glass frames.**

But the old town around the tree-lined Praza Xeneral Azcárraga and the Praza da Constitución, with its pale stone houses, romantic squares, churches and monasteries, feels bright and friendly compared to many town centres.

A large portion of the city is situated on a peninsula, which you can walk around via a long promenade. On the way, you will stumble across A Coruña's main landmark, the Torre de Hércules. Alongside this Greek hunk, a heroic woman also plays a lead role in the city's history: María Pita, the lady who lent her name to the arcade-lined main square in the centre.

WHERE TO START?

At the **Praza María Pita** you'll be spoilt for choice! You just need to decide which of this central square's archways you want to go through: you can either head to the sea where there are promenades backed by glass-filled façades; to the old town; or to shopping heaven. The bus and train stations are just 20 minutes away via Line 5. Car parks: Aparcadoiro Marina Parrote, Los Cantones or Palexco.

SIGHTSEEING

AQUARIUM FINISTERRAE 👪

Here you can sniff what fish and sea-food smell like before they end up on your plate; you will learn how waves are formed and where the water goes at low tide; and you'll find out what a crab's genitals look like. There are cute seals in the outdoor pool, who are so vain they'll pose for your photos for minutes on end. *March–Dec daily 10am–7pm, July/Aug until 8pm; Jan/Feb Mon–Fri 10am–6pm, Sat/Sun 11am–7pm | 10 euros, children 4 euros | Paseo Alcalde Francesco Vázquez 34 | coruna.gal/mc2/es | ⏱ 1½ hrs*

CASA DE LAS CIENCIAS 👪

If you want to see a Foucault's pendulum in action, you've come to the right place. This interactive science museum, located in a former palace, is great fun – and not just for kids. You can push things, shove things, swing things, press things and much more, all (somehow) in the name of physics. After all that hard work, you can relax in the digital planetarium. *March–Dec daily 10am–7pm; July/Aug until 8pm; Jan/Feb Mon–Fri 10am–6pm, Sat/Sun 11am–7pm | museum and planetarium 2 euros each, children 1 euro each | Parque de Santa Margarita | coruna.gal/mc2/es | ⏱ 1½–2 hrs*

CASA MUSEO EMILIA PARDO BAZÁN 👜

Come on in and make yourself at home! This time it's the former residence of author and feminist Emilia Pardo Bazán (1851–1921). The place

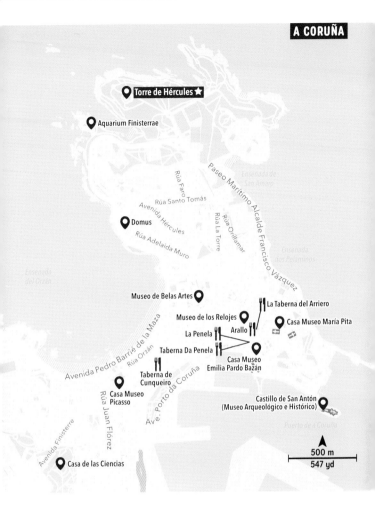

Torre de Hércules ★

Aquarium Finisterrae

Paseo Marítimo Alcalde Francisco Vázquez

Ensenada de San Amaro

Rúa Faro

Rúa Santo Tomás

Avenida Hércules

Domus

Rúa Oriñamar

Rúa La Torre

Rúa Adelaida Muro

Ensenada del Orzán

Ensenada dos Patamoiros

Museo de Belas Artes

La Taberna del Arriero

Museo de los Relojes

Arallo

Casa Museo María Pita

La Penela

Avenida Pedro Barrié de la Maza

Taberna Da Penela

Rúa Orzán

Casa Museo Emilia Pardo Bazán

Taberna de Cunqueiro

Casa Museo Picasso

Ave. Porto da Coruña

Rúa Juan Flórez

Castillo de San Antón (Museo Arqueológico e Histórico)

Puerto de a Coruña

Avenida Finisterre

Casa de las Ciencias

500 m
547 yd

has a cosy living room and study complete with family photos on the mantelpiece, as if the señora had just popped out to the shops. The museum is closed until further notice due to renovation work, but you can take a virtual tour on their website. *Rúa Tabernas 11 | casamuseoemiliapardo bazan.org*

CASA MUSEO MARÍA PITA 🐷

Heroine from A Coruña, María Pita (1565–1643) was married and widowed four times. But that's not what she's famous for. When the Spanish Armada had the bright idea of invading England in 1588, things famously went horribly wrong. The British fleet under the command of Sir Francis

Drake launched its counter-offensive in 1589 and A Coruña was one of its first targets. Although outnumbered, the Galicians managed to repel the invaders. According to legend, this was only possible because the women – notably María Pita – threw themselves into the fray. Head to her museum to learn about this exciting story and its historical context. The place is also furnished according to an inventory list of Señora Pita's home, making it an even more worthwhile visit. *Tue–Sat 11am-1.30pm and 6–8pm, Sun noon–2pm | free admission | Rúa de Herrerías 28 | coruna.gal | ⏱ 30 mins.*

CASA MUSEO PICASSO 🐷

This is the apartment where a young Pablo Picasso lived between 1891 and 1895. And this is where he learned to paint (at least, that's what they claim). The wall cabinet and sink in the kitchen date back to that time, while the rest of the details, including paintbrushes and palettes strewn around, are replicas imitating the style of the era. The museum is on the second floor of the building, and you need to ring the bell downstairs and climb a steep set of stairs. *Tue–Sun 11am-1.30pm and 6–8pm, Sun noon–2pm | free admission | Rúa Payo Gómez 14 | coruna.gal | ⏱ 30 mins*

INSIDER TIP
Imagine the young genius at home

CASTILLO DE SAN ANTÓN (MUSEO ARQUEOLÓGICO E HISTÓRICO)

Clay, rocks, broken fragments… A Coruña's archaeology museum has everything you would expect from, well, an archaeology museum. But the building itself is a sight to behold! Situated on an islet, this late 16th-century fortress once served as a prison. It's hard to believe - it feels so idyllic here now. Inside the fortress walls there are green lawns and lush hydrangea bushes; from the accessible roof of the chapel you have a great view of the sea; and the cistern below in the vault has a mystical feel to it. *Sept–June Tue–Sat 10am-7.30pm,*

Torre de Hércules

Sun 10am-2.30pm; July/Aug Tue–Sat 10am–9pm, Sun 10am–3pm | 2 euros | Paseo Alcalde Francesco Vázquez | coruna.gal | ⏱ 1 hrs

DOMUS 👼

Indoor playground or museum of humanity? Domus, which looks like a flying saucer from the outside, is very interactive. You can stand inside a beating heart, make a sound on the zebra crossing from the legendary cover of the Beatles album *Abbey Road*, score goals, and guess the belly-buttons of Britney Spears or Justin Timberlake. Sound confusing? It is. But it's great fun playing around with the 200 or so exhibits! *March–Dec daily 10am–7pm, July/Aug until 8pm; Jan/Feb Mon–Fri 10am–6pm, Sat/Sun 11am–7pm | 2 euros, children 1 euro | Rúa Ángel Rebollo 91 | coruna.gal/ mc2/es | ⏱ 1½–2 hrs*

MUSEO DE BELAS ARTES

The Museum of Fine Arts is well designed, but it's missing some big works of art. Nevertheless, you're bound to be captivated by Goya's series of engravings *Los Caprichos, Los Desastres, Los Disparates* and *La Tauromaquia*. The man clearly loved donkeys. Aside from these, other works are also quite entertaining. *Tue–Fri 10am–8pm, Sat 10am–2pm and 4.30–8pm, Sun 10am–2pm | 2.40 euros | Rúa Zalaeta | museobelas artescoruna.xunta.gal | ⏱ 1–2 hrs*

MUSEO DE LOS RELOJES 🐦

If you're interested in ticking wall clocks and grandfather clocks, this is

the museum for you. For everyone else, the splendid town hall where the timepieces are located is well worth a visit it itself. The venerable and stylish building includes a picture gallery, an impressive assembly hall, salons and the mayor's office. Warning: you need ID to enter. *Mon–Fri 5–7pm | free admission | Praza de María Pita | ⏱ 45 mins*

TORRE DE HÉRCULES ⭐

A young Picasso called this A Coruña landmark "Caramel Tower". If you make it up the 234 steps, you may be lucky enough to have the view all to yourself – lots of visitors give up before they get to the top. The oldest working lighthouse in the world is Roman in origin, probably from the first century, and it's protected by UNESCO World Heritage. Access to the top is limited to 17 people per tour and 30 minutes maximum. Booking in advance recommended. *Daily 9.45am–5pm, June–Sept 10am–9pm | 3 euros, 🐦 Mon free | torredehercules acoruna.com*

EATING & DRINKING

ARALLO

Trendy tapas bar with inventive dishes – and Michelin agrees. *Closed Mon/ Tue | Praza María Pita 3 | no reservations | arallotaberna.com | €€*

LA PENELA

Trim restaurant with traditional Galician cooking and views of both the sea and the Praza María Pita. *Closed Sun evening and Tue | Praza*

Shellfish galore – including three types of octopus – are on the menu in A Coruña

María Pita 12 | tel. 9 81 20 92 00 | lapenela.com | €€

LA TABERNA DEL ARRIERO
Quaint and rustic with giant portions of tasty *langostinos* for incredibly reasonable prices. And they're friendly here too. *Closed Tue/evening and Sun | Rúa Capitán Troncoso 19 | tel. 9 81 97 96 92 | FB | €*

TABERNA DA PENELA
The *tortilla de Betanzos* is famous and is ordered by the tonne. But steer clear of the *caldo galego* unless you like the taste of dishwater! *Closed Mon | Praza María Pita 9 | tel. 9 81 20 19 69 | tabernadapenela.com | €-€€*

TABERNA DE CUNQUEIRO
Cosy, informal place with a pub atmosphere and the most delicious *empanadas. Daily | Rúa Estrella 22 | tel. 9 81 21 26 29 | atabernadecunqueiro. com | €€*

SHOPPING
Loads of shops including a surprisingly large number of shoe shops can be found in the streets around the *Mercado da Praza de Lugo*. The market itself sells both fish and other more long-lasting local specialities. The *Rúa Riego de Agua* by the Praza María Pita is also a popular shopping destination. Daring fashionistas should be sure to purchase some designer Galician

NIGHTLIFE

Sophisticated culture and classical music (but some pop too) can be enjoyed at the *Palacio de la Ópera (Glorieta de América | palaciodela opera.com)*. The same goes for the *Teatro Rosalía de Castro (Rúa Riego de Agua 37a | FB)*. It's worth visiting just for the magnificent 19th-century building. Indie fans should check out the moody *Pub Lebowski (Rúa Trabajo 13 | FB)*, while night owls will also love *Patachim (Rúa Orillamar 16 | FB)*. Traditional Galician live museum can be found at *A Repichoca (Rúa Orillamar 13 | FB)*. And there are loads of bars and pubs in Rúa Orzán and the surrounding area.

clogs from *Eferro (Rúa Riego de Agua 4)*. And you'll find plenty of charming gadgets at *Greca Concept Store (Rúa Panaderas 18)*. For long-lasting accessories made from regional materials, try *D-Raiz (Rúa Pío XII 1)*.

BEACHES

A Coruña has four beaches. The smallest one, the *Praia das Lapas*, is 70m long and lies at the foot of the Torre de Hércules. Not much bigger is the 105m-long *Praia de Santo Amaro*, which is a favoured spot for sun-worshipers. The largest ones are the 570m city beach *Praia Riazor* along the promenade and the 700m *Praia Orzán* right next to it.

AROUND A CORUÑA

🄶 BETANZOS

25km southeast of A Coruña/25 mins via the AP 9

Betanzos (13,000 inhabitants) looks like the setting for a medieval action film. Three Gothic churches, monasteries, noble palaces, arcades – and all perched up on a hilltop. Animal lovers should visit the tomb of Count Fernán Pérez de Andrade in the church of *San Francisco*: his coffin rests on a wild boar and a bear.

We don't particularly recommend what is supposedly the town's main tourist attraction: the *Parque del Pasatiempo*, which was built in 1914 by the returning *Indiano* brothers García Naveira as a kind of whimsical pleasure garden with exotic sculptures, water features, columns and arches. However, the park is rotting away and has been closed indefinitely. Meanwhile, a new part of the park has been built opposite and it's dreadfulness knows no bounds. What a shame! ⧉ *D4*

🔲 FERROL

50km northeast of A Coruña/45 mins via the AP 9

The centre of Ferrol (73,000 inhabitants) is a major challenge to find, even with a satnav. If you don't lose your nerve driving through this rabbit warren of a city, you'll find yourself by the huge industrial docks and an equally huge shipyard, as well as a charming city centre with many glass-enclosed balconies – and plenty of vacant buildings too. But Ferrol has a major image problem: it is the birthplace of the dictator Francisco Franco, whose house has two commemorative plaques on it to remind us of the fact. You should probably refrain from asking the locals for the address (it's *C/ María 136*), as some of them might get prickly about it.

> **INSIDER TIP**
> **A rather dubious address**

When driving into Ferrol, it's worth taking a detour to the *Castillo de Andrade (Easter–Oct daily 11am–2pm and 4.30–7.30pm, mid-June–mid-Sept until 8.30 pm | 1 euro, ☞ Mon free)*. The stairs up to the battlements of the small fortress (1380) are mighty steep and should only be attempted by experienced stair-climbers. But the fabulous view of the Rías Altas is well worth it! ⧉ *D3*

> **INSIDER TIP**
> **A view of (almost) all the Rías Altas**

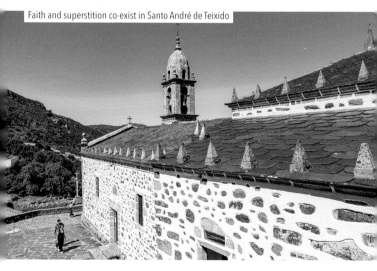
Faith and superstition co-exist in Santo André de Teixido

🖪 SANTO ANDRÉ DE TEIXIDO 🚩

95km northeast of A Coruña/1½ hrs via the AP 9 and AC 566

The only way to get to this miniscule pilgrimage site (50 inhabitants) is via lonely, winding tracks. If it's foggy, which it often is here, you won't see your hand in front of your face. And you definitely won't see the wild horses that are always walking out in front of cars. But the village itself is chock full of visitors, with pilgrims arriving in droves. According to the legend, if you don't make it here in your lifetime, you'll have to come back after death. The pilgrims are here to pay homage to St Andrew in a church dating back to the 16th century.

There's plenty of superstition on display in the church too, with offerings of arms, legs and baby dolls made of plastic or wax for the healing of broken limbs or fulfilment of a desire to have children. Most important of all are the *sanandresiños*, brightly coloured talismans made of bread dough, which are supposed to help you find love, friendship or success at work. 🕮 *D2*

🖪 CABO ORTEGAL

100km northeast of A Coruña/1 hr 40 mins via the AP 9 and AC 862

If you drive from A Coruña in the direction of Cabo Ortegal, you will understand why they say that parts of Galicia are dying out: the route is littered with partly or wholly abandoned villages. Often, you can hardly make out the *Se Vende* signs on the long-since dilapidated buildings. Even the pleasant port town of *Cariño*

with its colourfully painted houses is practically giving away real estate.

Behind Cariño is a narrow path leading to Cape Ortegal with its lighthouse. If you don't get blown into the sea by the strong wind, you will have a spectacular view of the Galician coast, rugged and beautiful with its sheer cliffs, right at the point where the Atlantic meets the Cantabrian Sea. On the way up to the cape, you can drink some deliciously cool spring water by the side of the road. 🕮 *D2*

INSIDER TIP
Fancy a cool drink?

🖪 VIVEIRO

115km northeast of A Coruña/1 hr 40 mins via the AP 9, AC 564 and LU 540

The whitewashed houses in the town's (15,500 inhabitants) *casco histórico* with their glass-enclosed gallery balconies are more reminiscent of Andalucía than Northern Spain. The best way to get to the old town is through the *Porta de Carlos V* (1548). This is where one of the biggest 🚩 Easter processions in Northern Spain takes place; you can see for yourself if you use the back door of the 12th-century church *Santa María del Campo*. Right in front of the door is a cluster of sculptures that resemble members of the Ku Klux Klan. Behind them are procession figures with the usual pained expressions. If you need divine assistance, there is a reconstruction of the grotto at Lourdes next to the 17th-century *Monasterio de la Concepción*, which will guarantee that your prayers reach the right ears. 🕮 *E3*

6 SARGADELOS ▸ ⬤

135km northeast of A Coruña/2 hrs via Viveiro

Galicia's famous porcelain factory, which is rather off the beaten track and looks from the outside as if it shut down long ago, is open to visitors who can watch the porcelain-makers at work. As well as the famous blue and white plates and cups, you can also buy amulets and charms that are supposed to protect you from witches and help you find love. *Mon–Fri 9am–3pm | free admission | sargadelos.com | ▯ E3*

7 PRAIA DAS CATEDRAIS ★ ⸙

150km northeast of A Coruña/1 hr 40 mins via the A 6 and A 8

If you're coming from Asturias, the fishing village of *Rinlo* offers the perfect introduction to Galicia's natural beauty. The *Ruta de las Playas* hiking route goes along the coast past five idyllic beaches: *Castros, Xuncos, Islas, Esteiro* and, the highlight, *Playa de las Catedrales*. The 1,300m beach gets its name from the rock formations shaped into vaults and arches by waves, wind and weather, giving you the impression that you're standing in a church.

The beach is only accessible at low tide and is completely flooded at high tide. And the tides come in quickly, so watch out! Warning: during Semana Santa and from July to September, you can only access the beach if you've booked in advance! You can do this at *ascatedrais.xunta.gal. ▯ F3*

8 ECOMUSEO FORNO DO FORTE ▸ ⸙ ⬤

45km west of A Coruña/40 mins via the AG 55 and AC 418

The unremarkable hamlet of *Buño* is famous for its pottery. Here, somewhat tucked away, you will find the region's open-air museum which has been furnished, down to the minutest detail, to resemble a 19th-century potter's house still very much in use by an *oleiro* family. You can go from room to room (there is a kiln right in the middle of the parlour, which explains the black ceiling). If you're in the mood for crafting, Tonio the potter will show you how it's done – and you can try it yourself. *Tue–Sat 11am–2pm and 4–7pm | free admission | Rúa Forno Novo | concellomalpica.com | ▯ B4*

9 SANTIAGO DE COMPOSTELA ★

75km south of A Coruña/1 hr via the AP 9

In addition to the hundreds of thousands of pilgrims that flock to Galicia's granite capital (97,000 inhabitants) all year round, tourists also swarm to the spacious *Praza do Obradoiro* where the cathedral can be admired in all its splendour and where the 15th-century former pilgrims' hospital Hostal dos Reis Católicos now houses one of Spain's noblest *paradores*. It's only a little less crowded on the neighbouring *Praza das Praterías* with its beautiful Fountain of the Horses.

If you want to see Santiago himself, head straight to the entrance of the *cathedral (daily 9am–8pm | catedraldesantiago.es)* and stand in line up the steps to the high altar, then wait (and wait… and wait) until it's your turn to embrace the statue of St James (hoping the person before you didn't kiss him too enthusiastically). Then you get into the next queue and wait (and wait… and wait) until you reach the crypt with the saint's remains, say a quick prayer and make your exit. It's also worth taking a look at the famous *botafumeiro*, an incense burner on a long rope weighing a total of over 50kg, which is swung up to the ceiling on special occasions, taking the strength of eight men. The Romanesque *Pórtico de la Gloria* from the 12th century is worth seeing too. The *Museo de la Catedral (April–Oct daily 9am-8pm; Nov-March 10am-8pm | 12 euros)*, featuring church treasure, lots of religious art and carpets, is attached to the cathedral.

For an insightful experience, visit the surprisingly contemporary *Museo das Peregrinacións e de Santiago (Tue–Fri 9.30am-8.30pm, Sat 11am-7.30pm, Sun 10.15am-2.45pm | 2.40 euros | Praza das Praterías 2 | museoperegrinacions.xunta.gal | ⏱ 1½ hrs)*, which provides information not just about the Way of St James but also about pilgrimage in general. There are also many bloodthirsty images of Santiago as a killer of Moors and Native Americans. According to legend, he came back down from Heaven when things got tough on Earth: firstly during the *Reconquista*, then during the colonisation of the Americas.

Before you escape the tourist hordes, be sure to take a detour into the *Museo do Pobo Galego (Tue–Sat 11am-6pm, Sun 11am-2pm | 4 euros | San Domingos de Bonaval | museodopobo.gal | ⏱ 2 hrs)*. Housed within the walls of an old Benedictine

The statue of St James on the high altar is the goal for pilgrims to Santiago de Compostela

Cabo Fisterra: not the end of the world, but the most westerly point in mainland Spain

monastery, the museum is organised into thematic rooms depicting Galician life, covering topics such as fishing, agriculture, crafts, music, etc. And if you're hungry, the *caldo galego* at traditional restaurant *Casa Carretas (closed Sun evening and Mon | Rúa das Carretas 21 | tel. 9 81 56 31 11 | restaurantecarretas.com | €-€€)* is quite something. *C5*

⑩ CARNOTA

100km southwest of A Coruña/1 hr 40 mins via the AG 55 and AC 400
This place is home to the longest ⚑ *hórreo* in Galicia – 35m long, made entirely from granite and dating back to the 18th century. To the uninitiated, these things look like sarcophaguses, but they are actually vessels, or granaries, for storing maize and cereals. The only thing is, the neighbouring town of Lira insists that their *hórreo* is a couple of centimetres longer. *B5*

⑪ CABO FISTERRA

110km southwest of A Coruña/1½ hrs via the AG 55 and AC 552
This is the final destination of the Way of St James, the westernmost tip of Spain and the end of the world, according to the translation of the original Latin term *finis terrae*. After arriving in Santiago, all self-respecting pilgrims walk the last 80km or so to get here (or they just pile on to buses). Either way, Cabo Fisterra is usually chock-a-block with people. But the nearby town with the same name (4,700 inhabitants) is pleasantly quiet.

The *castillo* on the edge of town, with its lovely garden, is home to the fishing museum, *Museo da Pesca de Fisterra (March–Dec Tue–Sat 11am–2pm and 4–6pm, June–Sept until 8pm, Sun 11am–2pm | 2 euros)*. But look out: if Señor Manolo starts talking at you in several languages about how smart a *pulpo* is, you'll never manage to get out of there. *A5*

VIGO

(□□ B6) **Vigo (294,000 inhabitants) has a busy shipyard, the largest fishing port in Spain and one of the largest commercial ports in the world. Here you can watch cruise ships being built or scrapped – and the uninititated amongst us can't always tell the difference.**

At first glance it might seem like an unattractive place. But as soon as you've eaten *empanadas* with hardened sailors by the docks or gulped down a few legendary local oysters, walked along the promenade by the marina or ambled through the small yet perfectly formed old town with its lively Praza da Constitución to the fishing neighbourhood of Berbés, as soon as you've sat on a terrace in the Praza de Compostela in the new town, dotted with sculptures and trees, Vigo will have won you over with its rugged,

WHERE TO START?

In a port city, the best place is the **harbour**! The marina is on the edge of the town centre. Parking spaces are scarce but the O Berbés car park in Rúa da Ribeira do Berbés usually has some space. From there, it's just a few minutes on foot to the waterfront promenade and the port where the island ferries set off, as well as the centre with its shopping areas. Vigo-Guixar station is also just a few hundred metres from the centre.

rough-around-the-edges charm. If not, just hop on a boat to the island nature reserve Islas Cíes with its pristine beaches.

SIGHTSEEING

MONTE O CASTRO
High up on the mountain you can walk through the ruins of a 17th-century fortification and enjoy an unparalleled view of the city, industrial zone and Ría de Vigo. And there's plenty of greenery to boot, since the place also includes a botanical garden and the remnants of the very first buildings from the second and third centuries BCE.

MUSEO DE ARTE CONTEMPORÁNEA DE VIGO MARCO 🐷
Historic on the outside, ultra-modern on the inside: the Museum of Contemporary Art, housed in a former prison and court (1880), shows temporary exhibitions, often featuring world-class artworks as well as up-and-coming local artists. *Tue–Sat 11am–2.30pm and 5–9pm, Sun 11am–2.30pm | free admission | Rúa do Príncipe 54 | marcovigo.com | ⏱ 1–1½ hrs*

MUSEO DO MAR DE GALICIA
In this maritime museum, which is laid out like a historical port, you will learn about Galicians' love of the sea and its history, from fishing and canning to crazy pioneer diving suits and a motley collection of ocean-themed toys, such as Barbie and Ken wearing

swimming costumes. *Mid-June–mid-Sept Tue–Sun 11am–2pm and 5–8pm; mid-Sept–mid-June Tue–Fri 10am–2pm and 4–7pm, Sat/Sun 11am–2pm and 5–8pm | 3 euros | Av. Atlántida 160 | museodomar.xunta.gal |* ⏱ 1½–2 hrs

PAZO DE CASTRELOS 🚩 🐖

The stately house stands in a delightful botanical garden, a haven for lovebirds cuddling up on benches. The house itself has some archaeological exhibits and many old but lesser-known masters. However, the interior of the *pazo* (palace) is worth seeing, as you will get a glimpse of what a fully furnished manor house looked like and understand how the Galician nobility lived in the early 20th century. *Pazo Tue–Fri 10am–2pm, Sat 5–8pm, Sun 11am–2pm; gardens daily 9am–8.30pm, May–Sept until 10pm | free admission | Parque de Castrelos | museodevigo.org |* ⏱ 2 hrs

VERBUM – CASA DAS PALABRAS 🐖

Is there anywhere that teaches about language more interactively than here? We doubt it! This "House of Words" has 29 giant multimedia cubes for you to mess around with – listen, speak and play. You'll learn loads about language, its origins and what you can use it for, from science to literature to advertising. The one downside: it's much less fun if you don't speak Spanish. *Tue–Fri 5–8pm, Sat/Sun noon–2pm | free admission | Av. de Samil 17 | verbum.vigo.org |* ⏱ 1–1½ hrs

EATING & DRINKING

BAR DORNEIROS

Be brave and head for the area by the docks: Alberto the fisherman serves up the freshest fish in town in a bar filled with hardened sailors and a rough-and-ready yet friendly atmosphere. The *plato del día* is unbelievably good value at 3 euros, and the *empanada* is unbelievably delicious. *Closed Sat/Sun | Av. de Beiramar 65, Espigón 3 | tel. 6 76 33 04 40 | FB | €*

> **INSIDER TIP**
> **Drink in that harbour atmosphere**

EL MOSQUITO

This traditional seafood restaurant has been in business since 1930. *Daily | Praza da Pedra 4 | tel. 6 16 50 45 44 | elmosquitorestaurante.com | €€–€€€*

EL TIMÓN

A simple, honest locale with a terrace, refined tapas dishes and friendly staff. *Closed Mon/Tue | Rúa Montero Ríos 6 | tel. 9 86 43 91 07 | €–€€*

LA TRASTIENDA DEL 4

Ultra-cosy restaurant with vintage charm and carefully curated, mostly Spanish cuisine with fusion elements. *Daily | Rúa Pablo Morillo 4 | tel. 9 86 11 58 81 | latrastiendadelcuatro.com | €€*

RÚA PESCADERÍA

In the mornings, when fresh oysters are delivered to this street, known locally as the *Calle de las Ostras*, and eaten then and there, this place is heaven. The nearby restaurants trying to lure in customers – not so much.

VIGO

El Timón

Rúa Pescadería | El Mosquito — The Othilio Bar — La Trastienda del 4

Rúa Carral

Rúa Policarpo Sanz

Rúa Colón / Rúa Colón

Museo de Arte Contemporánea de Vigo Marco

Rúa Cachamuiña

Rúa de María Berdiales

Rúa de do Ecuador

Rúa de Venezuela

Rúa de Bolivia

Avenida da Beiramar

Rúa Marqués de Valterra

Rúa de Pi y Margall

Avenida das Camelias

Rúa Hispanidade

Museo do Mar de Galicia

Verbum Casa das Palabras

Bar Dorneiros

Monte O Castro

Pazo de Castrelos

250 m
273 yd

Rúa de Vigo

Porto de Vigo

Ría de Vigo

THE OTHILIO BAR

Hip, modern, delicious and affordable. In other words, you'd better book in advance! *Closed Sun/Mon* | *Rúa de Luis Taboada 9* | *tel. 9 86 19 00 17* | *FB* | *€€*

SHOPPING

You can find big brands and elegant boutiques along the chic *Rúa do Príncipe* and the surrounding area. Restaurants and regional specialities can be found at the *Mercado O Berbés* in the square of the same name.

BEACHES

The popular 1.7km beach *Playa de Samil* is a little outside the centre to the south, followed by the smaller *Playa O Bao*. Both have a promenade running along them.

NIGHTLIFE

At night, the fishing quarter Berbés transforms into a party zone. If you like American kitsch, head to *20th Century Rock (Rúa Areal 18 | FB)*. For dancing and live music, try *La Casa de Arriba (Rúa Martín Codax 23 | FB)*. *Juke Box (Rúa Heraclio Botana 4 | FB)* enjoys cult status (partly for its gin and tonics).

AROUND VIGO

🔢 ISLAS CÍES ⭐

40 mins by ferry from the marina in Vigo

Between March and October, boats set off several times a day from the jetty at the marina to the Islas Cíes nature reserve, which is part of the *Parque Nacional de las Islas Atlánticas de Galicia*. The most popular destination is *⁎ Playa de Rodas* on the island of Cíes, which, with its turquoise water and Caribbean feel, was voted the most beautiful beach in the world by the *Guardian* newspaper. If you don't feel like taking a dip, follow the footpaths up to the lighthouse.

If the boats to Cíes are already booked up, you might still nab a seat on the ferry to *Isla de Ons*, another great place for sunbathing and hiking. Either way, book in good time via a company such as *Naviera Mar de Ons (Rúa Cánovas del Castillo | tel. 9 86 22 52 72 | mardeons.com)*, because daily visitor numbers are capped. 🗺 B6

🔢 BAIONA ⭐

25km southwest of Vigo/40 mins via the PO 552

You'll get the best view of this seaside town (12,000 inhabitants) from the 15m-tall monument of the *Virgen de la Roca (daily 11am–2pm and 4–9pm | 1.50 euros)* on *Monte Sansón*. The Virgin is holding a ship in her hand, and you climb up to the top via a very narrow spiral staircase. Only attempt this if you have a head for heights and are fairly slim! There's a walk that goes via an old *fortress wall (daily 10am–10pm | 1 euro)* round the *parador* on the Monterreal peninsula, where you can see as far as the Islas Cíes.

Aside from its 4km beach and historic old town, Baiona is known for being the port where the caravel 🔭 *La Pinta* docked, the first of three ships that Columbus brought back to Europe on 1 March 1493 after discovering America. You can climb on this replica, and there are even a few sailors still on board *(call tourist information for opening times, tel. 9 86 68 70 67 | 2 euros)*. You can find further information about the *Pinta* and seafaring in general at the *Casa de la Navegación (Tue–Sat 10am–1pm and 4–7pm; June–Sept 6–9pm | 2 euros | Rúa Ventura Misa 17 | museos.xunta.gal)*.

In the streets behind the beach and harbourside promenade, primarily in the *Rúa Ventura Misa*, you'll find countless bars and restaurants, including the upmarket *Casa Rita (daily | Rúa Carabela La Pinta 17 | tel. 6 77 06 83 65 | casarita.eu | €€–€€€)*. 🗺 B7

🔢 A GUARDA & SANTA TREGA

55km south of Vigo/1 hr via the AG 57, PO 340 and PO 344

The Río Miño separates Portugal from Galicia's southernmost town *A Guarda* (10,500 inhabitants), which is famous for its lobster. *Monte Santa Trega* is actually more interesting than the town itself. The sparse demarcations along the narrow, winding path to get there are reminiscent of gravestones

A 40-minute ferry journey to another world: Islas Cíes

– rather fittingly, perhaps, as the road can be highly dangerous when it's foggy. You'll come across a Celtic settlement with its origins in the fourth century BCE, whose round houses would once have been home to 5,000 people. Behind the settlement, the steep climb continues along a Way of the Cross up to the 17th-century *Ermita Santa Trega*, perched on the hilltop, and the *MASAT* archaeological museum *(mid-Feb-Dec Tue-Sun 11am-5pm; July/Aug until 8pm | 1.50 euros | museos.xunta.gal)*.

In the wine town of *Rosal*, 5km to the north, there is a steep, bumpy walk over hill and dale, which leads to the *Muiños do Folón e Picón*, 67 minuscule watermills, some in the form of tiny staircases, positioned one behind another along little streams. *□ B7*

INSIDER TIP
Wander up to miniature watermills

🔟 CASTILLO DE SOUTOMAIOR

25km northeast of Vigo/30 mins via the AP 9, N 552 and N 550

In the middle of a botanical garden resembling a park with trees up to 800 years old and countless camelias and hydrangeas, you can cross a drawbridge to the little 12th-century fortification that was converted in 1870 into a chic summer residence by the family of the Marqués de la Vega de Armijo. Inside you will find a ladies' gallery with a fantastic view and, next to it, you can look through the holes in the latrines and see where the nobility would have relieved themselves. A multimedia exhibition tells the story of the *castillo* and also explains that Columbus was actually Galician. *May-Sept daily 10am-9pm; Oct-April Tue-Sun 10am-7pm | 5 euros, garden free | castelodesouto maior.com | □ C6*

16 PONTEVEDRA

*30km north of Vigo/30 mins via the
AP 9*

The capital (83,000 inhabitants) of Galicia's smallest province is famous for its medieval old town with several aristocratic houses and lovely squares filled with bar terraces. The prettiest and most lively is the *Praza da Leña*, which also has two good restaurants, the *Eirado da Leña (closed Mon evening and Sun | tel. 9 86 86 02 25 | eiradoeventos.com | €€)* and the *Loaira (closed Sun evening | tel. 9 86 85 88 15 | €)*. A significantly larger square, the *Praza da Ferraría*, is dominated by the church of San Francisco. A few metres away is the *Santuario de la Virgen Peregrina*. The floor plan of this unique late 18th-century building, which is somewhere between Baroque and Neoclassical, is shaped like a scallop shell. ⟨⟩ *C6*

17 POIO

*30km north of Vigo/30 mins via the
AP 9*

On the opposite bank of the Río Lérez to Pontevedra, the ☛ *Casa Museo Cristóbal Colón (Wed–Sun 12–7pm | free admission | Praza Cristóbal Colón | turismopoio.com)* in the municipality of Poio offers definitive proof that the famous seafarer was not Italian but Galician. Why else would Columbus have named so many places in America after Galician *rías*? Why did he correspond in Galician? Why was the *Santa María* built in Pontevedra? And where did a man of slender means get the dosh for such an expensive expedition? Well, because he was in fact the illegitimate son of a Galician nobleman – or so they claim here.

You can visit some parts of the idyllic *Mosteiro de San Xoán de Poio (Mon–Sat 10am–1.30pm and 4.30–8pm, Sun 4–8pm | 2 euros)*, which has a Baroque church and a 16th-century cloister and is located at the other exit to the town. There is some very unusual regional art on display in the former dining hall. That rather suits the friars here, who swap their habits for T-shirts and the occasional earring. The monastery shop sells red and white wine made by the *fraíles*, as well as the Galician pomace brandy ⚑ *orujo*. ⟨⟩ *C6*

18 SANXENXO

*45km north of Vigo/50 mins via the
AP 9 and PO 308*

Galicia gets mass tourism too! In the summer, over 100,000 holidaymakers take up residence in Sanxenxo (17,000 inhabitants). There's a crowded beach *A Lanzada* (although it is 4km long!), plenty of hustle and bustle, discos, bars and pubs offering everything a pleasure-seeker could possibly want. ⟨⟩ *B6*

19 O GROVE & ILLA DA TOXA

*70km north of Vigo/55 mins via the
AP 9, AG 41 and VG 4.1*

There are around 70 beaches in and around ★ O Grove (12,000 inhabitants). The way to the peninsula leads either via a wooden walkway along the *Praia da Lanzada* or along a narrow road through dunes and mudflats. The various hiking trails are excellent for birdwatching. The main town of the

INSIDER TIP
Set sail for seafood

same name is famous for its seafood and fish. You can take a tour on a catamaran, which includes a mussel-tasting *(crucerosdoulla.com, crucerospelegrin.com)*.

While there are loads of fish restaurants here, a relaxed laid-back ambience is the order of the day. Many people say the best place in the square is the *Culler de Pau (Thu–Mon for lunch, Fri/Sat also for dinner; July/Aug Wed–Mon lunch and dinner | Rúa Reboredo 73 | tel. 9 86 73 22 75 | cullerdepau.com | €€€)*. The *Marisquería Solaina (daily | Av. Beiramar | tel. 986732969 | marisqueriassolaina.es | €€-€€€)* also sells plenty of seafood. For delicious fish with excellent wine to go with it, try *D'Berto (closed Mon evening and Tue apart from July/Aug | Av. Teniente*

Domínguez 84 | tel. 9 86 73 34 47 | dberto.com | €€€). At *Taberna Lavandeiro (closed Sun evening and Mon | Santo Antonio 2 | tel. 9 86 73 19 56 | €-€€)* the price is right as well as the quality.

You can skip the mediocre *Aquarium (acuariodogrove.es)*. You're better off heading straight to the *Museo da Salga (Tue–Sun 10am–2.30pm and 4.30-7pm | 2 euros)*, directly opposite. In the open-air part of the museum, you can find out how fish were salted and cured in the 18th and 19th centuries. The main building next door has an exhibition of fishing nets, small boats and beds, which seemed to be everything a person needed in life back then.

The elegant white bridge (1806) that leads from O Grove to the islet of *A Toxa* says it all: this is where the people with deep pockets spend their

Praza da Leña is the most charming square in Pontevedra

The ruins of Santa Mariña Dozo can be found on the outskirts of Cambados

holidays. There's a golf course, security guards, casino, beach club and a neatly tended little grove of trees beside a private villa… Mere mortals head instead for the quirky 19th-century *Capilla de San Caralampio* – which is decorated all over with scallop shells. *B6*

⑳ CAMBADOS ★

55km north of Vigo/45 mins via the AP 9, AG 41 and VG 4.2

The "capital of Albariño" on the Ría de Arousa has a beautiful historic centre with plenty of ⚲ *bodegas* to try out. The highlight is the 16th-century *Palacio de Fefiñanes*, a group of medieval buildings that have been preserved in their entirety and currently house the *Bodega Fefiñanes* (fefinanes.com). Information about the local white wine can be found in the lovely *Museo Etnográfico e do*

Viño (Mon–Fri 9am–2pm | 1 euro | Av. da Pastora 104). The nearby 🐦 *cemetery* is home to the ruins of the Santa Mariña Dozo church. Inside, the wife of Spanish author Ramón del Valle Inclán, who spent many summers here, is buried along with their young son who died in a tragic accident on the local beach. After visiting the graveyard, you can pick your spirits up with some delicious seafood at somewhere like *A Taberna do Trasno (closed Tue | Rúa Príncipe 12 | tel. 9 86 52 49 88 | atabernado trasno.com | €-€€)*. *B6*

㉑ VILANOVA DE AROUSA

60km north of Vigo/50 mins via the AP 9, PO 300 and PO 530

The bay in this town (10,000 inhabitants) is connected to the beach via a long footbridge. There are several sculptures in the centre that show how proud the town is of its most famous son. And in the middle of the small historic old town stands the *Casa Museo de Valle Inclán (summer Tue-Sun 10am-2pm and 5-9pm; winter 10am-2pm and 4-7pm | 3 euros | Rúa Luces de Bohemia | museos.xunta. gal | ⏱ 45 mins)*, the birthplace of the Spanish author Ramón María del Valle Inclán (1866–1936). Some of the original furnishings remain, along with film clips, photographs and works by the author, and the garden is an idyllic paradise.

Boats depart on excursions *(amare turismonautico)* from the harbour of the popular holiday island of *Illa de Arousa*, allowing you to get up close and personal with the fishermen and watch them at work. 📍 B5

22 PADRÓN

70km north of Vigo/50 mins via the AP 9

Almost everyone has heard of this place, even if they don't realise it: Padrón is the home of *pimientos de Padrón*, which have become something of a staple on menus in half of Europe. It is said that the ship carrying the body of the Apostle James once docked here at a *pedrón*, a Roman milestone. This is why all tourists make a pilgrimage to the church of *Santiago Apóstol*, where the *pedrón* is kept.

The town's other sights are mostly for bookworms: Padrón is where the famous Galician poet Rosalía de Castro (1837–85) spent her last years. Her former home, complete with her belongings, has been converted into a

lovely little museum, the *Casa de Rosalía (July-Sept Tue-Sat 10am-2pm and 4-8pm, Sun 10am-1.30pm; Oct-June Tue-Sat 10am-1.30pm and 4-7pm, Sun 10am-1.30pm | 2 euros | Aldea A Matanza | rosalia.gal/a-casa-museo | ⏱ 1 hr)*.

Camilo José Cela (1916–2002) should be better known internationally. The winner of the Nobel Prize for Literature in 1989 was born in Padrón. In the ⛱ *Fundación Camilo José Cela (Mon-Fri 10am-2pm, July-Sept also 4.30-8pm | 3 euros | Ortsteil Iria Flavia | fundacioncela.gal | ⏱ 1-1½ hrs)* you can find his manuscripts and personal belongings, as well as objects he felt compelled to collect – some of them quite bizarre. They range from glass eyes from the Spanish Civil War to snapshots of Picasso and Hemingway or the author's chamber pot collection. His Nobel Prize medal is also on display. If you want to visit Cela himself, he is buried in the cemetery behind the church opposite, under the third olive tree from the right. 📍 C5

INSIDER TIP Find Señor Cela under a tree

DISCOVERY TOURS

Do you want to get under the skin of the region? Then these discovery tours provide the perfect guide. They include advice on which sights to visit, tips on where to stop for that perfect holiday snap, a choice of the best places to eat and drink and suggestions for fun activities.

❶ A DAY IN THE PICOS DE EUROPA

➤ On the trail of the Spanish *Reconquista* in Covadonga
➤ Energetic hike to Enol and Ercina highland lakes
➤ Pooh – that stinks! Taste the famous Cabrales blue cheese

📍	Ribadesella	Llanes
→	135km, including 8km hiking route	1 day (around 2½ hrs total driving time)

ℹ️ There is limited access to the **Cueva de Tito Bustillo** in ❶ **Ribadesella**, so book online *(centrotitobustillo.com)*. It is also recommended that you book in advance for the cheese tour in ❹ **Arenas de Cabrales** either by phone *(tel. 9 85 84 67 02)* or online *(fundacioncabrales.com)*.

Lago de la Ercina is popular hiking destination in the Picos

INSIDER TIP
Sweets fit for a queen

Start in ❶ Ribadesella ➤ p. 88. Gather your strength in Queen Letizia's favourite holiday destination by munching on a sweet treat that bears her name. After you have enjoyed your calorific delicacy while ambling through the streets of the old town and along the harbour, visit the Cueva de Tito Bustillo *on the way out of town.* The guided tour of the cave – a designated UNESCO World Heritage Site – with its almost 20,000-year-old rock paintings, takes a good half-hour, but you have to be at the entrance 30 minutes beforehand or they won't let you in! After you've admired the rocks from the inside, it's time to head into the mountains proper. *The next stop is* ❷ Cangas de Onís. In the former capital of the Kingdom of Asturias, take a walk over the Puente Romano, the "Roman bridge", which actually dates back to the 14th or 15th century. Admire the giant Victory Cross that hangs from the bridge, harking back to that golden era.

A LEGENDARY BATTLEFIELD
Through deep valleys and densely wooded hillsides, follow the path as it leads up to the pilgrimage site ❸ Covadonga ➤ p. 94, where the Battle of Covadonga

❶ Ribadesella

26 km

❷ Cangas de Onís

11 km

❸ Covadonga

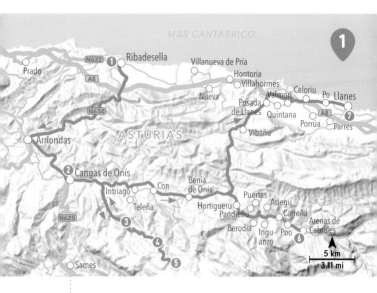

was fought in CE 722, instigating the *Reconquista*. In the Cueva Santa, the Holy Grotto, light a candle at the sarcophagus of King Pelayo, the conqueror and Asturian ruler. Then head to the imposing pilgrimage church nearby to send up a quick prayer to heaven.

Don't skip that prayer, because this is where the route gets trickier: *directly behind the sanctuary winds a steep, treacherous road next to a sheer drop at a height of 1,000m.* Watch out: dense fog can descend suddenly out of nowhere up here. If that happens, you won't be able to see other road users or free-roaming cows and donkeys, let alone the sheer drop. *After around 7km, you can park by the viewpoint* ❹ Mirador de la Reina.

8 km

❹ Mirador de la Reina

ON FOOT TO THE MOUNTAIN LAKES

Now you'll need to put on your walking books: *walk a good 4km, climbing around 100m in altitude to the* ❺ Lagos Enol y Ercina. When you get there, take a moment to enjoy the fantastic scenery with the mountains and lakes, and head for a well-earned food stop at Refugio Vega de Enol *(daily | tel. 6 99 48 85 44 | refugiovegadeenol.com | €)* where you can try dishes

4 km

❺ Lagos Enol y Ercina

like ⚑ *fabada,* a typical Asturian bean stew. *Head back to the car and return to Covadonga, where you can continue on to* ⑥ Arenas de Cabrales ➤ p. 95.

45 km

⑥ Arenas de Cabrales

SEEK OUT SOME STINKY CHEESE

In this village nestled in a valley, take a guided tour through a natural cave that is used to ripen the legendary blue Cabrales cheese – and try some samples too, of course. Finish off your day in the mountains by *heading back down to the sea towards* ⑦ Llanes ➤ p. 89. In this port, you can stroll through the picture-perfect medieval old town, where you can enjoy a sundowner and get stuck into a ⚑ *tapeo,* a tour of the tapas bars.

35 km

⑦ Llanes

② CYCLING THROUGH SANTANDER

➤ Enjoy maritime elegance at the marina
➤ Don your swimsuit and head to Bikini Beach
➤ Treat yourself to some local oysters

📍 Jardines de Pereda

🚩 La Mar Oysters & Drinks

➡ Around 15km

🚲 1 day (around 1 hr total cycling time)

ℹ Bring your swimming things and book a surfing taster session: *El Sardi (Tel. 9 42 27 03 01 | escueladesurf sardinero.com)*

In the morning, *head to the bike station at* ① Jardines de Pereda and hire a bike from *Tusbic (tusbic.es).* Then, if you're facing the sea, *head right and cycle to the industrial and fishing docks of Barrio Pesquero, where you should go to a quayside bar such as* ② El Muelle *(daily from 9.30am | Av. Sotileza 36)* and enjoy your first coffee of the day; or – like a hardened sailor – order a *carajillo,* an espresso with a shot of rum. Then continue *back along the seafront and the Jardines de Pereda to* what used to be the fishing docks and is now the

① Jardines de Pereda

2 km

② El Muelle

2½ km

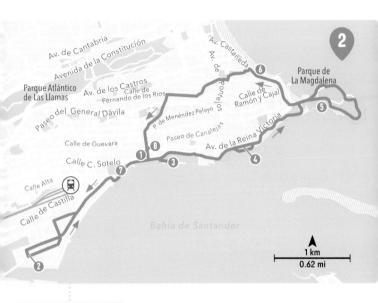

marina: ③ Puertochico. Once there, take a seat on a bench, enjoy the sunshine and wait for the effects of the *carajillo* to wear off.

SURF AND SEAFOOD

As soon as you've recovered, *continue cycling along the promenade to* ④ Museo Marítimo del Cantábrico ➤ p. 61, where you'll learn about Cantabria's relationship with the sea and meet a preserved giant squid. If you fancy your sea creatures a little fresher, head to the museum's restaurant with ocean view for a *menú del día. Next, cycle straight on until you reach the* ⑤ Península de la Magdalena ➤ p. 62. Relax awhile on the Playa de los Bikinis, enjoy the view of the grand palace (from the outside will do) and have a chat with some sea lions at the Parque Marino. Yes, it really is possible: just stand there and shout. They will hear you and respond!

DITCH THE BIKE AND RIDE THE WAVES

Now you can head a little further to the next beach, the ⑥ Playa El Sardinero ➤ p. 63. Here you can take a surf lesson or two with El Sardi *(Balneario 1a)* or hire a surfboard directly. *Next, slowly make your way back towards the centre and cycle via the Av. Hoteles, Bajada de la Encina, C/ Fernando de los Ríos and C/ Francisco Palazuelos to the Jardines de Pereda.* Drop off your wheels and head into the ❼ Centro Botín ➤ p. 61 for an artistic and cultural experience. Finally, walk to ❽ La Mar Oysters & Drinks ➤ p. 63, to enjoy some Cantabrian oysters in style.

❸ SANTIAGO & ITS SURROUNDINGS (FOR NON-PILGRIMS)

- ➤ Did you witness St James in drag?
- ➤ Sneak a peek at mysterious tombstones
- ➤ Go for a saunter in the "Versailles of Galicia"

📍	Santiago de Compostela	🏁	Santiago de Compostela
🔄	A good 230km	🚗	1 day (around 4 hrs total driving time)

Start your day in ❶ Santiago de Compostela ➤ p. 108 with a sumptuous breakfast buffet *(book by calling tel. 9 81 58 16 34)* at the San Francisco Hotel Monumento *(Campillo de San Francisco 3 | sanfranciscohm.com),* an abbey that has been ingeniously repurposed into a hotel. Then head to the Museo do Pobo Galego to ogle historic domestic objects and clothing, and to visit the grave of Galicia's cult poet Rosalía de Castro in the Pantheon.

SASHAY AWAY

Now head to your car and drive west to ❷ Corcubión. This relaxed holiday resort, with its heritage-protected old town and beautiful harbourside and beach promenade, is home to the 14th-century Iglesia de San Marcos, where you can admire a very weird depiction of Santiago wearing a kind of scallop bra and a robe with a long slit in it. Then, *continue on the AC 550 to* ❸ Carnota ➤ p. 110, where you can make a detour to

the longest hórreo (granary) in Galicia, dating back to the 18th century. *Next, drive along the seafront via Lariño and Louro – what are the odds you'll be tempted to take a dip as you drive past beach after beach on this stretch of coastline?*

MUROS, THE MUSSEL METROPOLIS

4 Muros

16 km

Soon you will arrive in **4** Muros *on the ría of the same name, with its medieval town centre that has been almost completely preserved.* Keep an eye out for all the *bateas*; these rafts floating near the shore are a dead giveaway that this place is famous for its mussels. You have to try them, of course, so why not head to the Restaurante Muradana *(daily | Av. Castelao 99 | tel. 9 81 82 68 85 | hotelmuradana.es | €€).*

28 km

This is where things get a little spooky: *continue along the ría* and you will reach the less-touristy **5** Noia where you can witness a strange sight: in the cemetery some 500 gravestones dating from between the 10th and the 14th centuries bear no name, and instead are engraved with puzzling pictures and symbols. Among

5 Noia

61 km

Carnota is the location of the longest *hórreo* in Galicia; it's a grain store on stilts.

the graves you will find the 14th-century church of Santa María a Nova, which houses even more gravestones in its mystical interior.

WE SAVED THE BEST TILL LAST

Last but not least, there's the ❻ Pazo de Oca *(daily 10am–2pm and 4–8pm, Nov–March 3–7pm | gardens 10 euros, with palace 20 euros | fundacionmedinaceli. org)*, which can be reached *via Padrón and Pontevea*. The origins of this country estate date back to the 13th century, while the gardens are from the 18th century. You ring the bell at the gate, pay your fee and enter a world of rose gardens, idyllic pergolas, fountains and two lakes featuring stone boats planted with flowers. It could hardly be more beautiful and romantic – it's not for nothing that the *palacio* is known as the "Versailles of Galicia"! After seeking refuge in this oasis of calm, the crowds of pilgrims *back in* ❶ Santiago de Compostela will be easier to bear.

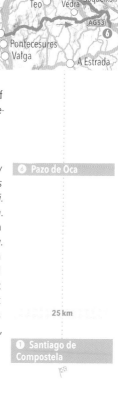

❻ Pazo de Oca

25 km

❶ Santiago de Compostela

④ THE BASQUE COAST HINTERLAND

➤ Seek out the little-known museum at the heart of heavy industry
➤ Visit a real *caserío*, a traditional Basque farmstead
➤ Learn about Ignacio de Loyola, the founder of the Jesuit Order

📍 San Sebastián

🏁 Santuario de Loyola

➡ Around 110km

🚗 1 day (around 2½ hrs total driving time)

ℹ Book your visit to the museum ❸ **Chillida Lantoki** *(lenbur.com)* in advance by calling *tel. 9 43 73 04 28.*

① San Sebastián

15 km

② Idiazábal

21 km

③ Chillida Lantoki

13 km

④ Oñati

9 km

This tour starts in ① San Sebastián ➤ p. 44, where you will *head south. On the way to the hinterlands, stop off in* ② Idiazábal *and buy some provisions in the shape of some tasty sheep's cheese. Enjoy the beautiful mountain and forest scenery all around you until, in the midst of this scenic idyll, you will find yourself at the heart of Basque heavy industry in Legazpi.* There, in a former paper factory, you will come across the lesser-known little sister of the Chillida Leku museum, the ❸ Chillida Lantoki *(visit by appointment, tel. 9 43 73 18 95 | 5 euros | Azpikoetxe Kalea | lenbur.com)*. Here you will learn what made the most famous Basque artists tick.

INSIDER TIP
Top tip for art fanatics

④ Oñati, *which is a further 20 minutes of winding roads away,* is in some ways the Oxford of the Basque Country, with the oldest university and bombastic Renaissance architecture. If you have a sweet tooth, check out the 🍫 chocolate museum Txokolateixia *(Sept–July Mon–Thu 10.30am–1.30pm and 5–7pm, Sat 10.30am–1.30pm, Aug Mon–Sat 10.30am–1pm | free admission | C/ Kale Barria 29 | oñatiturismo.eus)* – 200 years ago, Oñati was the mecca of Spanish chocolate-making with seven families active in the trade.

A little further south, surrounded by mountains, you will find the ❺ Santuario de Arantzazu (1955). Arantzazu has been something of a refuge for Basque people: a place of culture, identity and protection against the dictatorship. The blocky building is a matter of taste, but the surrounding area is amazing for hiking or just chilling.

Next, back to the countryside with 16th-century 🚩 farm museum ❻ Caserío Igartubeiti *(March–Oct Tue–Sat 10am–2pm and 4–7pm, Sun 10am–2pm, Nov–Feb Tue–Sun 10am–2pm, Sat also 4–7pm | 3 euros | Ezkio bidea | igartubeitibaserria.eus)*; the information centre in *Ezkio* explains what *caseríos* are and why the Basques are so fond of them. Lastly, another holy spot: the magnificent basilica in *Azpeitia*. The ❼ Santuario de Loyola, complete with Jesuit college, looks like St Peter's Basilica in miniature. Why so showy? Well, this was where Ignacio de Loyola (1491–1556), founder of the Jesuit Order, was born. His birthplace *(Nov–June daily 10am–1pm and 3.30–7pm, July–Oct 10am–6.30pm | 4 euros | loyola.global)* is still standing and open to visitors.

❺ Santuario de Arantzazu

29 km

❻ Caserío Igartubeiti

23 km

❼ Santuario de Loyola

GOOD TO KNOW

HOLIDAY BASICS

ARRIVAL

GETTING THERE

If you're travelling by car, the route from northern France passes via Paris and Bordeaux to the Spanish border at Irún. Most French and Spanish motorways are subject to tolls.

The best way to get to Northern Spain by plane is to fly to Bilbao, Santander or Santiago de Compostela. Ryanair *(ryanair.com)* offers direct flights to Santander and Santiago from London Stanstead; Spanish low-cost airline Vueling *(vueling.com)* has flights to Bilbao from London Gatwick and to Santiago from London Stanstead. Flights take around two hours. You can also fly to smaller *aeropuertos* in Northern Spain such as Vigo or A Coruña, but these usually involve a transfer in Barcelona or Madrid.

Making the journey by train is expensive and time-consuming, and involves travelling from London to Paris, Paris to Hendaye, and Hendaye/Irún to San Sebastián *(seat61.com)*.

The ferry is a popular way to travel from the UK to Northern Spain. Brittany Ferries *(brittany-ferries.co.uk)* operates three routes: Portsmouth to Santander; Plymouth to Santander; and Portsmouth to Bilbao.

The bus company Flixbus *(flixbus. co.uk)* also travels from London to Bilbao (via Paris). The journey takes about 23 hours and costs around £50.

CLIMATE & WHEN TO GO

Northern Spain is notorious for its unfavourable weather. It certainly can get very hot in the summer, but it can experience serious storms in autumn and winter. The Spaniards take their holidays in July and August, so everything will be busy then and

You'll find beach life and farm life side by side at Playa de Oyambre in Cantabria

accommodation will be booked up or overpriced. The best time to travel is from April to June, or in September and October. Hardy souls can swim anytime between the end of May and the end of October, but wimps should stick to the weeks between late June and late September.

GETTING AROUND

CAR

The speed limit in built-up areas is 30kmh (50km/h on multi-lane roads); outside urban areas, the limit is 90km/h where there are no signs to the contrary; and 120km/h on motorways. Stick to the speed limits or else you could face a hefty fine. The breath alcohol limit is 0.25 milligrams per litre (0.15 for new drivers), which roughly corresponds to a blood alcohol limit of 0.5 milligrams per litre. The fine for using a mobile phone while driving is 100 euros. Spaniards and rental car drivers must carry two warning triangles in their cars; foreign cars are exempt. Both local and foreign cars are required to keep a reflective vest in the car and you must wear it if you break down or get a flat tyre and need to get out of the car while on the road.

You can park for free in zones marked in white, but you pay to park in the blue zones. If you park where you're not supposed to, your car may be been towed away and you will have to pay 200 euros for its release.

Spanish motorways are divided into *autopistas de peaje (AP)*, which are subject to tolls, and *autovías (A)*, which are similar to motorways but toll-free. The narrow roads of the Picos de Europa are best suited to small cars, but they're often so steep that you'll need an SUV to get up them.

PUBLIC TRANSPORT

All the major towns and cities in Northern Spain can be reached easily and relatively cheaply by train (*renfe. es*). Or why not treat yourself to a trip on the luxury *Tren Transcantábrico (eltren-transcantabrico.com)*, which runs along the coast from San Sebastián to Santiago?

Another option is the Spanish long-distance bus network, which has myriad routes, works like clockwork and charges reasonable prices. For example, you can get from San Sebastián to Gijón for 30 euros. One of the main providers is Alsa (*alsa.es*).

EMERGENCIES

EMBASSIES & CONSULATES
UK EMBASSY
Torre Emperador Castellana, Paseo de la Castellana 259D, 28046 Madrid | tel. 9 17 14 63 00 | www.gov.uk/world/spain

US EMBASSY
Calle de Serrano 75, 28006 Madrid | tel. 9 15 87 22 00 | es.usembassy.gov

CANADIAN EMBASSY
Torre Emperador Castellana, Paseo de la Castellana 259D, 28046 Madrid | tel. 9 13 82 84 00 | international.gc.ca/ country-pays/spain-espagne/madrid. aspx?lang=eng

HEALTH
The European Health Insurance Card (EHIC) is accepted for EU visitors. Everyone else needs adequate travel insurance. In the event of illness, head to the local *centro de salud*, where the emergency department will be called *urgencias* or *emergencias*. Pharmacies are called *farmacias* and can be identified by a green cross.

EMERGENCY NUMBERS
Emergency number for police *(policía)*, fire brigade *(bomberos)*, ambulance *(ambulancia)* and other emergency services: *tel. 112*

ESSENTIALS

BEACHES
Not for nothing does Galicia's *Costa da Morte*, or Death Coast, bear its name. But the same name could be applied to the coastline along the rest of Northern Spain, where many of the beaches have treacherous currents, so you must never swim out too far and should preferably stick to beaches with lifeguards. Lifeguard season usually

FESTIVALS & EVENTS
ALL YEAR ROUND

JANUARY
Tamborrada (photo, San Sebastián): 24-hour drum parade, *danborrada. donostiakultura.eus*

MARCH/APRIL
Semana Santa (e.g. in Viveiro): Holy Week processions.

APRIL
Fiesta de La Folia (San Vicente de la Barquera): Procession of sailors.

MAY–JULY
Rapa das Bestas: Catching wild horses in the mountains of Galicia.

JULY
Feria de Indianos (Colombres): Festival of *Indianos*.
Festa da Langosta (A Guarda): Lobster festival, *turismoaguarda.es*
Jazzaldia (San Sebastián): Jazz festival, *jazzaldia.eus*
Semana Negra (Gijón), Festival of literature and culture, *semananegra.org*

AUGUST
Fiesta del Albariño (Cambados): Wine festival, *fiestadelalbariño.com*
Batalla de Flores (Laredo): "Battle of the Flowers", a procession with spectacularly decorated floats, *batalladeflores. net*
Festival Internacional Santander (Santander): Festival of music and dance, *festivalsantander.com*
Descenso Internacional del Sella (Arriondas): Canoe festival, *descensodelsella.com*
Romería Vikinga (Catoira): Viking battle and giant booze-up at the Torres de Oeste castle ruins, *catoira.gal*

SEPTEMBER
Internationales Filmfestival (San Sebastián): *sansebastianfestival.com*

OCTOBER
Fiesta del Marisco (O Grove): Seafood festival, *turismogrove.es*

starts at the beginning of June and lasts until mid/late September. The general rule is: if you see a green flag, it's safe to swim, yellow means proceed with caution, and red means absolutely no swimming. The *Bandera Azul*, or blue flag, on the other hand, is used on beaches that are particularly environmentally friendly and have good facilities. Going topless is fine, but getting completely nude is frowned upon (except on official naturist beaches).

CUSTOMS

Goods for personal use can be freely imported and exported within the EU. This covers up to 800 cigarettes and 10 litres of spirits, for example.

For government limits on quantities of alcohol, tobacco and other goods that that can be brought back into the UK, see *gov.uk*. For US regulations, see *cbp.gov*.

HOW MUCH DOES IT COST?

Coffee	*1–1.40 euros for a cortado*
Tapas	*2–5 euros for a tapa or pintxo*
Wine	*1–1.50 euros for a small glass*
Petrol	*around 1.65 euros for 1 litre of super*
Football ticket	*from 30 euros for a match at Athletic Bilbao*
Surf lessons	*from 30 euros for a one-day course (around 2 hrs)*

INFORMATION
TOURIST OFFICES

In the UK: *Heron House, 10 Dean Farrar St, London SW1H 0DX (by appointment only)* | *tel. 020 7317 2011*

In the US: *60 E 42nd St, New York, NY 10165* | *tel. +1 212 265 8822*

In Canada: *2 Bloor St W, Toronto, ON M4W 3E2, Canada*

TOURIST INFORMATION ONLINE

Useful websites: *spain.info* (official Spanish tourism portal)
turismoasturias.es (Asturias)
tourismus.euskadi.eus (Basque Country);
turismo.gal (Galicia)
turismodecantabria.com (Cantabria)

OPENING TIMES

In Spain, there is no set closing time for shops. Most shops open Monday to Saturday between 9.30 or 10am and 1.30 or 2pm and then from 4.30 or 5pm to 8pm (sometimes they only open in the morning on Saturdays). Banks and government offices are usually only open in the morning. In major tourist destinations, many shops will stay open all day until late evening in peak season, and large supermarkets and shopping centres skip the siesta too.

PUBLIC HOLIDAYS

Some regions also celebrate 19 March and 25 July. If the public holiday falls on a Sunday, the following Monday is often taken as a holiday.

1 Jan	Año Nuevo (New Year's Day)
6 Jan	Reyes Magos (Epiphany or the Three Kings Festival)
March/April	Jueves Santo (Maundy Thursday) and Viernes Santo (Good Friday)
1 May	Fiesta del Trabajo (Labour Day)
15 Aug	Asunción de la Virgen (Assumption of Mary)
12 Oct	Día de la Hispanidad (National Day of Spain)
1 Nov	Todos los Santos (All Saints' Day)
6 Dec	Día de la Constitución (Constitution Day)
8 Dec	Inmaculada Concepción (Immaculate Conception)
25 Dec	Navidad (Christmas)

TELEPHONE

The country code for Spain is 0034; for the UK it's 0044; for the USA and Canada it's 001.

There are no area codes within Spain, so you always need to type the full nine-digit number. Thanks to the EU's roaming reform, EU nationals won't be charged extra for making calls or surfing the net. Non-EU nationals need to check with their provider to see what is covered in their contract.

TOILETS

Toilet facilities in Spain are much better than they used to be. But it's a good idea to carry tissues or wet wipes with you, just in case paper is not provided.

WEATHER IN BILBAO

■ High season
■ Low season

	JAN	FEB	MARCH	APRIL	MAY	JUNE	JULY	AUG	SEPT	OCT	NOV	DEC
Daytime temperature	12°	14°	15°	16°	20°	22°	25°	25°	24°	21°	16°	13°
Night-time temperature	5°	6°	6°	8°	10°	13°	15°	15°	14°	11°	8°	7°
Hours of sunshine per day	2	3	4	4	5	6	6	6	5	4	3	2
Rainy days per month	14	13	12	13	12	8	6	7	8	10	12	13
Sea temperature in °C	12°	12°	12°	12°	14°	16°	19°	20°	19°	17°	15°	13°

☀ Hours of sunshine per day   🌧 Rainy days per month   ≋ Sea temperature in °C

WORDS & PHRASES
IN SPANISH

SMALL TALK

yes/no/maybe	sí/no/quizás
please/thank you	por favor/gracias
Hello!/Goodbye/See you soon	¡Hola!/¡Adiós!/¡Hasta luego!
Good morning/evening/night	¡Buenos días!/¡Buenas tardes!/¡Buenas noches!
Excuse me/sorry!	¡Perdona!/¡Perdone!
May I?	¿Puedo …?
Sorry?/Could you repeat?	¿Cómo dice?
My name is …	Me llamo …
What is your name? (formal/informal)	¿Cómo se llama usted?/¿Cómo te llamas?
I am from … the UK/USA/Ireland	Soy del Reino Unido/de los Estados Unidos/de Irlanda
I (don't) like this	Esto (no) me gusta.
I would like … /Do you have …?	Querría …/¿Tiene usted …?

SYMBOLS

EATING & DRINKING

The menu, please!	¡El menú, por favor!
expensive/cheap/price	caro/barato/precio
Could you bring … please?	¿Podría traerme … por favor?
bottle/jug/glass	botella/jarra/vaso
knife/fork/spoon	cuchillo/tenedor/cuchara
salt/pepper/sugar	sal/pimienta/azúcar
vinegar/oil/milk/lemon	vinagre/aceite/leche/limón
cold/too salty/undercooked	frío/demasiado salado/sin hacer
with/without ice/fizz (in water)	con/sin hielo/gas
vegetarian/allergy	vegetariano/vegetariana/alergia
I would like to pay, please	Querría pagar, por favor.
bill/receipt/tip	cuenta/recibo/propina

MISCELLANEOUS

Where is …?/Where are …?	¿Dónde está …? /¿Dónde están …?
What time is it?	¿Qué hora es?
today/tomorrow/yesterday	hoy/mañana/ayer
How much is …?	¿Cuánto cuesta …?
Where can I get internet/WiFi?	¿Dónde encuentro un acceso a internet/wifi?
Help!/Look out!/Be careful!	¡Socorro!/¡Atención!/¡Cuidado!
pharmacy/drug store	farmacia/droguería
broken/it's not working	roto/no funciona
broken down/garage	avería/taller
Can I take photos here?	¿Podría fotografiar aquí?
open/closed/opening hours	abierto/cerrado/horario
entrance/exit	entrada/salida
toilets (women/men)	aseos (señoras/caballeros)
(not) drinking water	agua (no) potable
breakfast/B&B/all inclusive	desayuno/media pensión/pensión completa
car park/multi-storey car park	parking/garaje
I would like to hire …	Querría alquilar …
a car/a bike/a boat	un coche/una bicicleta/un barco
0/1/2/3/4/5/6/7/8/9/10/100/1000	cero/un, uno, una/dos/tres/cuatro/cinco/seis/siete/ocho/nueve/diez/cien, ciento/mil

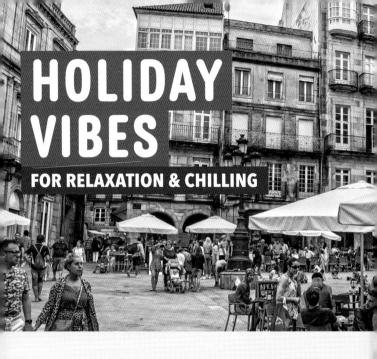

HOLIDAY VIBES
FOR RELAXATION & CHILLING

FOR BOOKWORMS & FILM BUFFS

📖 PATRIA (HOMELAND)
Fernando Aramburu's epic 2016 novel about the ETA terror campaign and the impact on society, which has since been adapted into a TV series. The story delves into the madness of nationalism and terrorism (and not just in the Basque Country).

🎬 DIECISIETE (SEVENTEEN)
Daniel Sánchez Arévalo's funny yet touching 2019 road movie about two very different brothers, a geriatric grandmother and a three-legged pooch against the backdrop of the breathtaking Cantabrian landscape.

🎬 OCHO APELLIDOS VASCOS (SPANISH AFFAIR)
The most successful Spanish box office hit of all time by Emilio Martínez Lázaro. It's about an Andalucían who falls in love with a Basque woman and, although it was released in 2014, it is still very, very funny, especially in the original or with subtitles.

🎬 RIFKIN'S FESTIVAL
In 2020, Woody Allen chose the San Sebastián Film Festival as the backdrop for his latest tale of fraught emotional relationships

PLAYLIST
RANDOM VIBES

0:58

II LUZ CASAL – PIENSA EN MÍ
Big ballad from this diva who was born in Galicia and raised in Asturias. Has had a cult following since Almodóvar's film *Tacones lejanos (High Heels)*.

► BAIUCA – MORRIÑA
This cool mix of folk-rock voices, Galician instruments and zippy electro vibes makes you want to get up and dance.

► RULO Y CONTRABANDA – DENTRO DE UNA CANCIÓN
The best of Cantabrian guitar rock.

► SÉS – CONCORDIAS DE PAPEL
Softer sounds from the Galician rock rebel.

► LA OREJA DE VAN GOGH – LA PLAYA
Soft and melodic song by this successful band from San Sebastián – like the end of a day at the beach.

Your holiday soundtrack can be found on **Spotify** *under* **MARCO POLO Spain**

Or scan this code with the Spotify app

ONLINE

KULTURALDIA.COM
Savvy online culture magazine about San Sebastián and the surrounding area. Only available in Spanish or Euskara (Basque).

SHORT.TRAVEL/SPA4
A well-made video about Bilbao's famous museum and the "Guggenheim Effect".

SMARTSANTANDERRA
From weather forecasts to beaches, cultural events, traffic and museums – this app contains pretty much all you need to know about Santander, Cantabria.

TRAVELCOOKEAT.COM
Marti Buckley is a cook and author living in San Sebastián, who blogs about food and lifestyle.

TRAVEL PURSUIT

THE MARCO POLO HOLIDAY QUIZ

Do you know what makes the North Spain Coast tick? Test your knowledge of the idiosyncrasies and eccentricities of the region and its people. You will find the answers below, with further details on pages 20–25 of this guide.

❶ What does the Centro Niemeyer in Avilés look like?
a) Like half a chicken egg
b) Like a stylised fish
c) Like a dying swan

❷ How many officially recognised variants of the Way of St James are there on the Iberian Peninsula?
a) Five
b) Seven
c) Nine

❸ What are the names of the two brown bears living in the Fundación Oso de Asturias?
a) Paca and Molina
b) Edurne and Jone
c) Tola and Juanita

❹ Which regional language has completely different roots to Castilian Spanish?
a) Galician
b) Basque
c) Asturian

❺ Where is the birthplace of Franco, the Spanish dictator?
a) Llanes in Asturias
b) Ferrol in Galicia
c) Santillana del Mar in Cantabria

❻ According to a survey, what are the most beautiful beaches in Northern Spain?
a) Catedrais, Concha, Rodas
b) Bikini, Laredo, Sardinero
c) Arnao, Poniente, San Lorenzo

Answers: 1a, 2b, 3a, 4b, 5b, 6a, 7b, 8c, 9a, 10c, 11b

Don't look at the caption until you've done the quiz! This is the Centro Niemeyer in Avilés

❼ Who do people in Northern Spain refer to as "Indians"?
a) Economic migrants from Latin America
b) Asturians who emigrated to America and returned having made their fortunes
c) Sporting Gijón footballers in red kit

❽ What is or was *Prestige*?
a) An urban development project to boost tourism in Santander
b) A premium hiking trail in the Picos de Europa
c) A tanker that capsized off the coast of Galicia

❾ What is Covadonga?
a) The site of a legendary battle
b) Traditional Asturian bagpipes
c) A typical Cantabrian pastry

❿ Where did the Spanish *Reconquista* start in the eighth century?
a) In the caves around Altamira
b) In Santiago de Compostela
c) In the Asturian mountains

⓫ Which part of the coast is called the *Costa Verde*?
a) The west coast of Galicia from Cabo Fisterra to the Portuguese coast
b) The Asturian coast
c) The eastern part of the Basque coast from San Sebastián to the French border

INDEX

WE WANT TO HEAR FROM YOU!

Did you have a great holiday? Is there something on your mind? Whatever it is, let us know! Whether you want to praise the guide, alert us to errors or give us a personal tip – MARCO POLO would be pleased to hear from you.
Please contact us by email:
sales@heartwoodpublishing.co.uk

We do everything we can to provide the very latest information for your trip. Nevertheless, despite all of our authors' thorough research, errors can creep in. MARCO POLO does not accept any liability for this.

PICTURE CREDITS
Cover photo: Cuevas del Mar (Schapowalow: R. Schmid)
Photos: Huber-images: M. Cassale (46), O. Fantuz (8/9), G. Gräfenhain (2/3, 40/41), R. Schmid (26/27, 126), R. Taylor (29); J. Karres Azurmendi (143); mauritius images: L. Avers (109), C. Magnon (110); mauritius images/age fotostock: G. Azumendi (83, 120/121), A. Carrera (55), J. Larrea (28/29), J. C. Muños (70), J. Nicolás Sánchez (37), M. Ramírez (21, 106), K. Zelazowski (front cover flap, inside front cover 1); mauritius images/Alamy: J. Alba (49, 62, 130/131), D. Carreño (117, 138/139), C. Castilla (56/57), T. Christ (67), A. Flórez (12, 72/73), M. Galan (115), D. Gato (14/15, 78), Hanmon (11), K. Hockenhull (94), P. Horree (33), C. Magnon (13, 96/97), H. Milas (10), C. Nandez (118), J. Ossorio Castillo (85), M. Ramírez (81, 89, 90), F. Troiani (16/17), L. Vallecillos (52), L. Vilanova (102); mauritius images/Alamy/Basque Country: M. Baynes (133); mauritius images/Alamy/Kpzfoto (65); mauritius images/Alamy/Mikel Bilbao Gorostiaga-Travels (140/141); mauritius images/Alamy/Peakscape (back cover flap); mauritius images/Alamy/Prisma Archivo (86); mauritius images/Alamy/ZUMA (34/35); mauritius images/John Warburton-Lee: P. Adams (104/105); mauritius images/Masterfile RM: J. Woodhouse (22); mauritius images/Onoky: D. Schneider (25); mauritius images/United Archives/WHA (69); mauritius images/Westend61: V. Barreto (32/33); Shutterstock.com: John Chica (6/7), Barmalini (30).

2nd Edition – fully revised and updated 2023
Worldwide Distribution: Heartwood Publishing Ltd, Bath, United Kingdom
www.heartwoodpublishing.co.uk

Authors: Susanne Jaspers, Jone Karres Azurmendi
Editor: Nikolai Michaelis
Picture editor: Gabriele Forst
Cartography: © MAIRDUMONT, Ostfildern (pp. 38–39, 122, 124, 127, 129, inner flap, outer flap, pull-out map); bilekjaeger; ©MAIRDUMONT, Ostfildern, using data from OpenStreetMap, Licence CC-BY-SA 2.0 (pp. 42–43, 45, 51, 58–59, 60–61, 74–75, 76–77, 93, 98–99, 101, 113).
As a publisher of tourism texts, we present only the de facto status of maps. This may deviate from the situation under international law and is wholly unbiased.
Cover design and pull-out map cover design: bilekjaeger_Kreativagentur with Zukunftswerkstatt, Stuttgart
Page design: Lucia Rojas

Heartwood Publishing credits:
Translated from the German by Rachel Farmer
Editors: Kate Michell, Rosamund Sales, Sophie Blacksell Jones
Prepress: Summerlane Books, Bath
Printed in India

MARCO POLO AUTHOR
JONE KARRES AZURMENDI

Since returning to Spain's Atlantic coast, German-Basque author Jone Karres Azurmendi has been spending her time either in the sea, on the Way of St James or in a *pintxo* bar, where she enjoys plying visitors with local delicacies and tasty Rioja and filming reports for German television. She loves films and is a serious foodie. She was also made a jury member for the annual blood sausage contest – and for good reason!

DOS & DON'TS

HOW TO AVOID SLIP-UPS & BLUNDERS

DON'T SMOKE ON THE BEACH
Cigarette butts in the sand are gradually becoming a thing of the past. As elsewhere, smoke-free beaches are growing more common in Spain. In Galicia alone there are already 141. You won't pay a fine for it yet, but it's still best to avoid lighting up.

DON'T TOUCH THE NIBBLES
Never, ever touch a *pintxo* on the counter and then put it back. That is a mortal sin and will draw the wrath of the restaurateur. The same applies, of course, to tapas if you're perched at the bar.

DO BE PATIENT WHILE DRIVING
In the hinterlands of Northern Spain, there are rural areas where the few (often very elderly) residents will drive slowly to the shops, taking their time along the winding switch-backs and narrow mountain roads. And you should do the same. Overtaking is extremely dangerous and, in any case, the landscape is far too pretty to rush.

DON'T TRUST SIGNPOSTS IN THE WILDS
Many places in the middle of nowhere have signs to supposed tourist attractions. Don't trust them! The paths often lead to dead ends or bumpy dirt tracks. And if you do end up at a historic ruin, it's likely to be barricaded shut.

DON'T TALK ABOUT THE POLITICAL PAST
It may sound weird, but not all Galicians saw Francisco Franco as a dictator. And there are some in the Basque Country who revere the members of ETA as heroes. So avoid these topics and talk about current politics instead. Most Spaniards are happy to laugh about that.